# The Whispering Hills of Thali

# The Whispering Hills of Thali

Krishna Yadav

DEV PUBLISHERS & DISTRIBUTORS
New Delhi

*Published by:*
**Dev Publishers & Distributors**
2nd Floor, Prakash Deep,
4735/22, Ansari Road,
Darya Ganj,
New Delhi-110002
Phone : 011-43572647
e-mail: devbooks@hotmail.com
website: www.devbooks.co.in

ISBN 978-93-81406-07-6
First published 2012



Printed in India

# Contents

# Chapter 1

She looked at the envelope marked 'Rajanaika Public School, Kasauli', and wondered why the school had sent her a special invitation at her new address in Shimla after over seven years of her having left school. She opened it. It was an invitation from the office of the Dean, Mr. Varma, to attend the forthcoming Founder's Day on 18th October and stay on for the the annual dinner for old students hosted by the alumni. She smiled, deciding to attend it for the first time since she'd left school so long ago, to meet old friends, to reminisce about the old memories of childhood and the growing years at the beloved school she had spent them. The years had been full of problems, happiness and sadness, but sharing those beautiful, carefree years with her close friends had surpassed all.

Turning to the side table next to her bed, she opened the first drawer and took out the small golden frame that held a photograph of a young, handsome boy with windblown hair who was astride a black stallion. He was wearing khaki Jodhpurs and was looking up at the mountain slope with a smile. The mere sight of the photograph was enough to make her heart race. Lying on her bed holding it in her hands, she recalled how she had fallen in love with him during the final year of school. Even after so many years that love persisted, rendering her unable to take an interest in any other man even when she had lived abroad in Australia and London.

Looking at the photograph, she recalled how Karan was so different from the other boys in the school. He was called "the royal" Karan, tall – about 5'11" – with an athletic body, a very fair, flawless, glowing complexion and a long face with sharp features. But best of all were his large brown eyes that looked at the other person with meaning when he smiled; there was a knowing mischeif behind them. He was not only good at sports like riding, playing polo, tennis, squash, or swimming, but known also for debating at school and the inter-state school competitions at Doon and Mayo, and he always held the first position in the school grades. No wonder he was admired by the crowd of friends, both boys and girls that he loved to be with, and also by all the teachers.

No one but her father knew about her love for him. Initially, he took it lightly because it was his only child's love, and that too, so early in life. But with the passing of the years, even he became convinced of it and promised her that he would never compel her to settle down till she desired it. This time on her return to India, however, he felt helpless before her mother in whose opinion she ought to be married by now so had asked her once again. But then on her insistence had once again promised to leave her lone till all was settled within her.

She looked at the clock – it was past 10 am – and decided to inform her nanny about the safe arrival of her parents at London and request her to make arrangements for the forthcoming trip to Kasauli on 16th October, and to inform her son Karmu, the caretaker of the cottage, to clean and get it ready for her short stay there. After dressing she left the room. All day long she was excited about the trip and reflected on the reasons of wanting to see Kasauli again so much. *Why haven't I ever attended this function after leaving the school?* she wondered. It could be because she had left her address with Karan but he had never contacted her. The mere thought made her think again, just as she had done all along after leaving school that it was not the friends, but one man in her life, Karan, that mattered. Yes, there seemed to be hope of meeting him again. His memory made her smile, but then came the thought that he could be a married man by now. A sudden depression overwhelmed her and all the excitement was no more. She thought *whatever it may be, at least this one-sided love that I've been nurturing for ever so long for this man will cease and hopefully I will become free and finally prepared for my future.* By end of the day, though, she knew that nobody could ever take his place in her life and she would never forget him, even if he by now was a married man. Yes, she had loved him all those years and would in the future too.

It was early evening when she reached the cottage named 'Krina Cottage' by her father and remembered how excited she had been, when she was driven to it for the first time at the age of ten. The cottage was situated just below the highest point of Kasauli's famous television tower, and though small with two bedrooms, it was compact and cosy. It was over seven years since she had come to this place and wondered why she hadn't visited it for so long. *Could it be because I was too busy? Or was it resentment or an attempt to avoid my past?* she wondered. Perhaps it was just that medical school life was too hard and most of the holidays were so limited that they had to be spent either in Dalhousie or Chamba with her parents. After that, she had moved to a distant land and forgotten everything except her love for her parents and Karan. Now standing next to the bay window of her bedroom on the first floor, she looked out to see a clear sky and a setting sun. The valley was slowly being engulfed in the shadow of evening, and soon there would be lights all around. So many years had elapsed since she visited Kasauli, which had been developed as a cantonment sanatorium by the English. The remote hill station located on the first high ridge of the Himalayan foothills had a view not of the dusty plains, but of the higher Himalayas that seemed to beckon. The English had selected the greater height, about 6325 ft above sea level, of Shimla to build their summer capital which they had developed after shifting the capital of the empire to Delhi from Kolkata in 1903.

How long she stood looking around she did not know. Even though dusk had settled, the view was still beautiful; lights were scattered all over the valley below and on the mountains surrounding it. She recalled how her parents started visiting Kasauli more often after purchasing the cottage from the Englishman, Mr. Steven Royal, who at first was determined to spend his retirement there but left for Glasgow in Scotland after the death of his Anglo-Indian wife, Rosi.

Krina was the only daughter of a rich timber merchant. The Khannas were a close-knit family of three and their very comfortable means kept them happy within themselves. By nature she was very quiet, aloof, and not outgoing. She loved to read and write poetry and to paint landscapes of hills. She had started horse riding at the age of seven and loved to ride with her father who was a keen rider himself. She also had a melodious voice, and a love for P*ahari* folk songs. She was good at lawn tennis, debating and always got a good position in her studies but had a reputation of being very quiet and stubborn. Those who didn't know her called her arrogant and proud.

Thinking of her parents visiting London made her smile. After thirty years her father would be reunited with his older brother and his family. She remembered the first time she visited Glasgow to meet her uncle, Dr. Surya Kumar Khanna and his wife Sakina. He mentioned how hurt he had been when his parents told him that since he had married a nurse, and that too a Muslim, it was best he stayed there rather than return to India. So he became a general practitioner and never visited India again, not even when his parents died. But now that he had had a heart attack he rang up his brother to come to Scotland because he wanted to see him. She knew how much her uncle was missing India when she first met him and saw his misty eyes. She loved her uncle and his beautiful wife and their son, Rohit, who was now a plastic surgeon. They both liked each other and though she had been working at Edinburgh, she visited them very frequently at Glasgow. So once again, the two Khanna families came very close.

The sudden cold breeze through the open window brought her back to the present and she looked at the clock. It was past 8 pm, and it was very dark so she decided to postpone exploring the old, memorable places of her past in Kasauli to the next day and take her dinner and some rest. She would attend the celebrations of Founder's Day on 18th October, the day after.

Krina knew that come Founder's Day this small, sleepy town would be humming with crowds of parents and children, and that laughter and music would break the serenity and solitude. The old memories of her as a young child anxious and keen to meet her parents on this day made her smile within. Unable to sleep after her meal, she decided to read and picked up a book on the Shimla Hills her father had given her when she was in high school. He had asked her why the hill station called 'Simla' earlier during the Raj was now changed to Shimla and then smiled at her ignorance. The very next day he bought this book and told her that one must know about the places one visits or lives in. When she began reading about Kasauli she was surprised that it, like Shimla, got its name from a village called Kasool. It was the royal summer retreat of the erstwhile ruler of the Beja Princely state. South-west of the city of Solan, Kasauli is situated on a hill over-hanging the town of Kalka with splendid views of hills and valleys, and is surrounded by dense forests of pine. It came to be known for its fragrance of pine, which lured many well-known people to settle there. In 1842, the English founded the army school station amidst the dense forest of tall trees of chir, pines, rhododendrons, willows, deodars and oaks. She recalled her weekend visits to their cottage where, regardless of the weather, she would climb the hill and stand at the highest point of the town, the television tower close to the cottage, and enjoy the breathtaking view in solitude. The mist would slowly roll down the slopes, sometimes thickly covering the panorama and sometimes lightly as though playing a game of hide and seek, making the view romantic and stunning. Kasauli, however, is best known for sunny days and even in severe winter is not too cold. She remembered climbing the slope in autumn and walking under the bare trees whose leaves covered the ground, to whose beauty and charm added the chirping birds. Her visits to the cottage became frequent on the weekends, when she could roam around, have a good dinner with the nanny and rest till Sunday evening.

She loved the life within her own cocoon away from friends, though it was short-lived because the school would close for winter vacations and she would have to leave with the nanny for Dalhousie. That town, her birthplace, represented happiness and togetherness of the Khanna family; the three of them enjoyed each other's company enough to keep it just among themselves. However, Dalhousie was unlike Kasauli, too cold and always shrouded in thick mist till late afternoon. Kasauli is still a military cantonment with tranquil trails winding up the hillside, quaint cottages that are reminders of the colonial era and lush, beautifully laid out gardens with delicate creepers and vibrant flowers that lend a fragrance to the air. Now there are many private houses owned by people as an escape from the heat of the plains. There is hardly any mist in early February and the days are sunnier, enabling a view of the snow capped peaks of the Shimla Hills in the north-east, which in the mornings are bathed in the golden rays of the sun. In fact, even most of the winter nights are clear and starry, which inspire her to compose poems and write in her diary. She remembered the river Sutlej flowing down the gorge like a snake to the north-west, beyond which, again, were mountains covered with dense forest of tall trees. She had always wondered why there wasn't any snow on the high peaks, but one could see snow-topped mountains if one stood at the Monkey point, which offered a good view of Dhaula Dhars, a range at a distance, with the 3643m high Choor-Chandini (Choor Dhar) immediately above the foot hills bathed in softly illuminating moon light. Choor Chandini is said to look like hundreds of silver bangles descending the snow slopes and thence it derives its name.

Her thoughts turned to her school, remembering the first time she discovered that Rajanaika Public School, Kasauli. It was founded by Rana Pratap Singh, the ruler of Saket dynasty in 1917. He was not only Rana but also a statesman who believed in providing education to the children of Indian soldiers serving in India as well as to children of those who gave up their lives serving the Raj. Every Ranahui, the children studying in the school called 'Ranahui' (Ranas), they were from upper caste Ranas, Thakurs and others also Anglo-Indians are a staunch believer of the school's motto of "Never relent – Fight for honour". Krina recalled the beautiful buildings on the separate hilltop at the elevation of about 5800 ft amidst a dense forest of pine and cedar. There were four houses: Everest, Kanchenjunga, Kailash and her house, Shivalik. Each house with its contingent of boys, girls and teachers lived like a joint family. Karan was the prefect of the house. He had a special selection of friends she was excluded from because of her quiet and reserved nature. She was often too engrossed in her studies, playing tennis, or busy composing poetry.

A knock at her door brought her back to the present. The nanny brought in the morning tea and drew back the curtains. Krina accepted the cup and looked out of the window. The sun had flooded the valley, and at the sight of the town below, she decided to enjoy the day outdoors by herself. She let the nanny know that she would be going to the Mall, and by the time she was dressed it was already past 11. She left dressed in a loose black *kurta* over tight *churidar* pyjamas and a red skivvy, with light green woollen cap to cover her head. Her shoulder-length hair was tied into a tight ponytail and she was wearing comfortable walking shoes. Kasauli had two Malls that encircled the town like a necklace, and two lanes led to the town in the shape of a capital H, one through the upper Mall and the other from the lower Mall. The lower Mall's 3 km stretch was lined with pine and oak trees. She decided to take the lower lane which was slightly narrow but cemented, and where one could find shelter from the sun under the canopy of tall trees. The narrow road was crowded with people she knew had come to attend the school's Founder's Day. She took in the fresh-scented pine aroma as she walked. The laughter, the chirping birds, the greenery and liveliness filled her with happiness and once again turned her thoughts to Karan, till she forgot everything except that this was the place she had first found love. She remembered his large brown eyes, his sardonic smile, their first kiss, and the picture of him sitting majestically on the stallion, and immediately the sobering thought returned that he couldn't possibly still be a bachelor.

She dispelled those thoughts and looked around at the town the authorities maintained so well. The houses along the narrow road were old-fashioned bungalows with secluded gardens, possibly still occupied by the same old families. Her father had told her that Kasauli was and still is a sought-after town for officers to retire and live in tranquillity and peace – peace that gives way once every year to the Founder's Day of the famous school that is now meant only for rich children from all parts of India. The school has attained its reputation in all fields of education, academic, and sports and games. The school has good facilities for both indoor and outdoor sports including a gymnasium and a heated pool. Since parents' attendance at the event is compulsory to please their children, they come in large numbers, crowding the small town.

Now she was strolling through the lower Mall's shopping centre. Unlike Shimla the shops were small but full of wares to attract both young students and also the local inhabitants. The standard of living in this quiet hill station is very high like the modern city of Chandigarh, so everything is available in the market to cater to the taste of rich children and the well-known inhabitants of the town. Kasauli has a club, St. Mary's church and the celebrated hotel Alisia which was built during the British era. As she reached the Mall, she noted with a smile that nothing had changed. There stood the Gupta store on the elevated mound behind the two pipal trees that was so popular with Ranahuis. It provided them with all the daily needs, freshly baked chocolates, biscuits and other treats to fill their pantries and hungry stomachs. She walked on to observe the courtyard flanked on either side by small shops and eateries like coffee shops, a chicken and kebabs restaurant, an ice cream parlour and fruit-chaat stalls.

The tables and chairs were placed outside the chicken shop so that one could take in the fresh breeze of this north-eastern Himalayan region while sitting under sunny, dusky, or even misty sky, enjoying the food. Moving towards the left, she avoided the Tibetan women sitting with their display of handmade woollens and beaded jewellery that used to attract her during her school days. She walked slowly towards her parents' favourite shop, Sharma Store. She climbed the two wooden steps and looked inside from the last step. Nothing had changed. Uncle Sharma, who always gave her chocolates and shared tea with her parents, was still there. She looked at the bespectacled man bending over some accounting work by the old register and smiled fondly at him. He was so old yet was still managing the shop. There was no one else within and she wondered where his son Deepak, her schoolmate was. He was very intelligent, and the last she had heard of him was that he was posted as deputy commissioner of Rampur. Deepak was an only son, adored by his family who were ready to sacrifice anything to make him a successful man. Krina admired their spirit.

The old man saw her and enquired, "What can I do for you?" in a Pahari dialect. She stepped inside and went close to him. Adjusting his spectacles, he recognised her and smiled, "My Krina, when did you come here?" He got out from behind the counter and hugged her.

"Yesterday", she replied and then said, knowing who he was looking for, "They have gone to London to see my uncle who underwent a heart operation!"

He laughed and said, "You've changed so much! You are a more beautiful and smart young woman now, but you still have the same innocent face that charmed my family and me. Oh, you must have some tea with me; it's getting cold here."

She accepted and told him that she was here to attend the Founder's Day and asked where Deepak was.

"He is married now and posted at Kangra," he replied.

"Oh, he must be visiting you often, uncle!" Krina continued.

"Well, once they settle down with their own woman, they have less time for the oldies." She did not miss the sadness in his eyes and the hollowness of his voice.

Adding a cheer to her own voice she said, "I came here to meet you and to buy something for myself, my nanny and her son, just like I used to."

He went behind the counter and said "You're my first customer this morning and I am confident you will be lucky for me." When she said she wanted to buy some Pashmina shawls in different colours, he pulled out a bundle and placed it on the counter for her to browse through. Then she asked him to show her some hand-knitted woollen caps and socks, of which she selected the red, green and blue caps and three pairs of black socks, and finally, she chose a mixed wool shawl for her nanny and a sweater for the nanny and Karmu each.

When the bill was presented, she looked in her bag and realised with embarrassment that she only had thousand rupee notes, and that Uncle Sharma might not have change so early in the day. However, he said, "Don't worry; I must have money from you to get customers and enjoy earning the whole day long. You sit at my desk and don't allow any customers to leave. I'll be back with your change," and left the shop.

She sat at the desk and gazed at the road outside which was now bustling with people, especially around the eateries. As her gaze alighted on the chicken shop, she saw a family eating chicken *tikkas*, she was reminded of an incident involving Karan.

She had always been fond of the chicken shop's salami sandwich and ate there often with her friends, Bimla and Kanta. One Saturday, the three were shopping at the Mall when Krina sat down to eat tikkas while her friends were still in a shop. She had sat at the very same table the family sat at, and heard a husky voice say, "So, the langur is non-vegetarian despite being a disciple of Hanumanji who was a vegetarian!"

She looked up to see Karan standing close, looking at her with that meaningful smile. He caught her by surprise because she had been confident that he would never tease her in the marketplace, but there he was.

Her heart sank as she looked around and realised they were surrounded by his friends, and would have no help. She decided to keep silent. "So the monkey has lost her tongue. Why?" He laughed, then put a small paper bag with monkey nuts and whispered, "I bought this for you, and I'm sure that you'll enjoy them just like the rest of your race." When she saw that he had turned around and walked away, she opened the bag and started eating the nuts, but his husky laugh made her look up again. He was standing by her side yet again, grinning at her sardonically, saying, "So the Pahari langur is hungry and happy to have her staple diet." Laughing loudly, he strode across the road and joined his friends. Embarrassed and red-faced, she could only watch.

She was so lost in her thoughts that she didn't hear the footsteps of a customer enter the shop till a soft cough brought her back to the present. A young white girl was looking at her with an enquiring smile.

"Oh, I'm sorry!" Krina apologised.

The customer smiled. "That's alright. You seemed to be lost in deep thought, in some pleasant dreamland, but my advice to you is not to lose yourself in dreams while working in the shop."

Guiltily, Krina replied, "Yes, I know."

"I'm glad to have found someone who speaks English. Please help me buy some woollen things. Do you have any Pashmina shawls?"

Krina fetched the shawls and placed them on the counter before her.

Her accent told Krina she was not English but American. "Are they pure wool?" she asked, spreading them on the desk.

"Of course," Krina replied, and studied her as she looked through the shawls. She wasn't too young but tall, about 5'11" or perhaps more, with blond hair and a long, flawless white face. Her features were sharp, but it was the pair of large blue eyes that added to her beauty. She had a siim, willowy figure and the light blue slacks with a deep green woollen polo-neck she wore showed her to be a woman with perfect taste in clothes, who knew how to use them to enhance her appearance and personality.

Krina almost lost herself in staring at her beauty with admiration and was brought back by another soft cough, leaving her red-faced with embarrassment.

The girl looked at her with a meaningful smile and said, "You're a daydreamer and that reddened, shy look adds to your beauty, but this habit is bad for your profession." She laughed, wrapped a light brown shawl around herself and went to the mirror. "Now look at me. I wish to have this shawl." Then she turned to the door and said in a slightly louder voice, "Please come in and tell me how this colour looks on me, Karan darling!"

# Chapter 2

The name made Krina perk up and to her utter surprise, she saw a man outside, bent on the last step, tying his shoelace. Panic overwhelmed her and her heart hammered against her chest. She still harboured the hope that somehow, it might turn out to be someone else with the same name. But all those hopes were quelled when he looked up. "Nancy, I think you should buy blue and green ones that bring out your eyes," he answered while entering the store and then winked at her.

"Oh Karan, you're a teaser. You really know how to please," Nancy laughed, her cheeks turning red. While she turned to choose more shawls, Krina wondered desperately how she could hide in the tiny shop. She tried to keep her face hidden from Karan by turning to the woman, but he walked up to them.

Karan was still the same, with short curly hair, those brown eyes, and the same athletic figure which had now become more muscular. He wore brown corduroy trousers with a matching tweed coat over a grass green skivvy. He stood close to the American woman till his gaze fell on Krina. He looked at her intently, and then leaned a little closer, smiling the same cynical smile as his eyes met hers.

The silence that followed made Krina grow nervous, finally broken by the woman. "Do you have it in blue?"

"No, we don't have blue in Pashmina wool," Krina said quickly.

"Oh, don't you?" Karan said, still staring at her.

"No," she replied, avoiding his gaze, "but you can have it in light green."

She picked up the green shawl and wrapped it around herself, saying, “Karan how does this look?”

Karan said with his smile, “Please, go ahead and buy all the colours you want, but do get a muffler, a Kulu cap and woollen gloves for me.” She looked at Krina and asked for the items. Then she turned to Karan, touched his elbow and asked, “What colour?”

“Blue and green,” he laughed. The girl blushed and Karan turned his face, still intently staring at Krina, who was in a fix. She didn’t know where everything was kept. “Hurry up!” he ordered.

She nodded and began looking at the shelf closest to her, but didn’t find them. Krina turned to the woman and requested, “Please just wait a few minutes for the owner to come; he’ll show you the things you asked for.”

She agreed but asked to be shown socks. In the meanwhile, Krina knew where the socks were, having purchased some herself, so she pulled out a bundle. While the woman busied herself looking through them, Karan leaned closer and said in a low voice, “You’re Krina, aren’t you? Why are you trying to avoid me? What a change.” She didn’t trust herself to reply. He looked her up and down with his sardonic smile. It brought back all the memories of being teased by him in the past, and she decided to put an end to it. She stared back defiantly, but Karan was unperturbed. “So you’re a salesgirl now? But you’re lousy at that, too, aren’t you?”

Now she was angry. “Don’t be rude, or...”

“Or what? What will you do to your customers who have bought so many things?”

“You’re being difficult!”

“Am I?”

“Yes,” she said, but when she looked at him again, she got lost in those large brown eyes. He stared back at her. How long they were lost, neither of them knew till the woman piped, “Darling!” and made him look up. “Nancy, look around; we’re going to have to wait for the owner to come and show us what we want. This lousy salesgirl is no good.” He turned to Krina once more with his smile and shining eyes. "Though you've changed, you're still ugly like a monkey, a Pahari langur, trembling like a kitten. Just look at yourself. I haven't even touched you, and you're still so scared of me. Lousy salesgirl. What a profession for a rich Ranahui."

The woman was now looking at a green woollen cap, modelling it in front of the mirror. Karan reached over and with a steel grip, held Krina's wrist. "You had once slapped me, remember? Then you laughed to insult me and made fun of me when I tried to tell you something to make up with you. Nasty Krina, I hated you and never forgot, all these years," he laughed, but it was a hollow laugh. Still gripping her wrist, he continued, "You've just rekindled the pain of that insult, but know one thing: Karan never forgets or bears an insult, especially from someone so ugly, a commoner beneath my status...a salesgirl." He tightened his hold.

"You're hurting me!"

"At this moment, I want to slap you so it'll always remind you of what you did to me."

"Go to hell!"

"Wild monkey-faced ugly Krina, I'm not going to be insulted again by an inferior woman!" with that he pushed her back and let go of her wrist.

Rubbing her wrist she looked at him. His face was red and his eyes blazing. Suddenly, he went over to where the woman was standing. "Pack up everything, draw up the bill and include your commission even though you don't deserve one for being so lousy. Fancy a salesgirl not knowing where what is in a shop."

The woman looked at Krina who was desperately looking out of the window to see if Uncle Sharma was coming, and said, "Don't worry; just pack the things that I have selected." She came close to Krina and noticed her kurta for the first time. "What a beautiful dress! Can I have one?"

"No, it isn't sold here."

Karan said daring Krina to respond, "It is sold here. Look at this woman, bent on ruining her employer's business with her ignorance!"

"Karan, what's wrong with you? You're being rude and insulting to the poor girl!"

"Am I? Well I'm not sorry because clearly she's unsuitable for the job."

Karan continued staring at her with hostility and Krina shifted uncomfortably. The woman watched her closely again and came up to touch her shoulder saying, "What an unusual dress! It really suits you!"

"Really, Nancy?" Karan said.

"Oh yes. It's so different from all the others that I have seen travelling from Delhi to here! Tell me about this dress, Karan."

"It's worn by tribals living high up in the Himalayas, nomads who love wearing gaudy clothes. They're called Gujjars and Gaddis. She's from one of those tribes," he sneered at Krina. "Stupid and lazy."

The woman turned to Karan and said, "Please don't be so rude; I want to buy one for myself."

"Of course! Worn by you, it'll enhance its charm unlike when it's worn by this miserable, ugly salesgirl."

"Karan," the woman warned.

"Show her the dress," he said to Krina, "though an expensive one, not like one to your taste: cheap. Look at the colour combination you're wearing – black, green and red!"

"I already told her, we don't sell dresses here," Krina replied.

"Even if you do, you probably aren't aware of it!"

"No, we don't have any and I am perfectly aware of it!" Knowing Karan, he was simply provoking her so she would look at him and talk.

He turned to Nancy and said, "On our way back, we will stop at Shimla and buy you one, and if you wish, we'll have more made in your favourite colours at Thali."

"Oh, thank you Karan," the woman softly kissed his cheek. Krina watched his face turn red and when he turned to the woman, saw that her face was flushed, too, though she looked as if she was glowing with happiness. It was evident that she was equally as much in love with Karan as he was with her. Sadness gripped her heart but she didn't let it reflect in her expression by turning to the window looking for Uncle Sharma, wondering at the reason for his delay. Then she took her place behind the counter without looking at the couple when Karan came close to her.

He took out his wallet and said, "Now pack everything up and make the bill. Don't forget to add your commission even though you don't deserve a single penny." The sarcastic and insulting way he said it infuriated Krina but she controlled her anger out of deference to Uncle Sharma whose customer he was. Watching her stormy face he laughed and said, "So you do get angry but you can't react because you have to save your job!"

She grabbed the bill and wondered what to do as she started writing down the items but didn't know the prices.

"Hurry up, or we'll leave without paying, though I'll be glad to hear that you have been sacked by your employer."

She heard Uncle Sharma's hurried steps at the door and heaved a sigh of relief. She left the desk and went to the door when he called out her name. "I'm sorry, but even the Gupta store couldn't help me," he explained, pulling out her bundle from the corner. "You're going to be working in Shimla now, aren't you? Well, you must see me before you leave," he said.

She thanked him and then confessed, "I tried my best to attend to your customers, but I'm not used to your job. I have no idea what's kept where or what the prices are. I did my best, but I do realise that I am an abysmal saleswoman." She smiled affectionately at him and touched his shoulder without looking at the couple clutching their purchases, ready to leave. Uncle Sharma blessed and hugged her before she left the store. As she walked out of the door, she heard him say, "Oh, Karan, she was not a saleswoman…" but she refused to listen to more. All she could think about was that the man she was so much in love with belonged to someone else. It was too late for her to repent now.

She was far too upset and lost in her thoughts to enjoy the beautiful walk back to her cottage. Even after so many years, Karan was still the same, as proud and arrogant as ever. She remembered their kiss, her first, and the one that had changed her entire life at such a young age. Yes, he was her first love and still held that position in her heart though he was with another woman now. She guessed they were married, judging by the intimate looks they had shared. The thought propelled her into dejection once again. She hadn't seen it before, but she was certain now what she had lost in the wait for Karan, and wondered how she would ever forget him; those brown eyes still made her lose herself in them every time he looked at her. Then something nagged at her: *why had he been looking so deep into my eyes?* She pondered over it for a while but couldn't quite figure it out.

As she lay in bed that night she took out the photograph once more and looked at him. He was still just as haughty as he had been then, in the way he held her wrist. She was so vulnerable, but she had felt no pain, only the excitement of his touch after so many years. The thought of slapping her took her back to the past when she tolerated his teasing at every corner of the school but lost her patience one evening when she had decided to swim in the heated pool. Someone had suddenly caught her from behind and holding her, planted a kiss directly on her lips. She had looked up and slapped him. She watched his face turn red and his large brown eyes bore into hers as he still held her in a tight grip. She grew scared but they were lost in the gaze they shared till suddenly, he slapped her back. He pushed her onto the floor and left her without another glance. As she watched him leave, she knew she was in love.

There was nobody at the pool for a while, so she was left to herself and her thoughts as she floated in the water on her back, filled with excitement. Other students began filing in soon, so she returned to her room. At dinner she looked for him but he was nowhere to be seen, not even among his crowd of admirers though they noted his absence. She kept wondering where he was and since she couldn't get any sleep till early morning she decided to look for him on the slope where he would return to from his morning ride.

On her way to the slope, someone called out to her. She turned to see her friend Bimla who asked, "Where are you going?"

"Why?"

"We all know he kissed you! It was a bet. He told all his friends that he could hold you and kiss you, and so he did," she blurted out. "Krina, I'm your friend and I'm going to advise you to stay away from him and save yourself further humiliation." Krina saw Karan coming but she turned and ran towards her own room.

She knew she was in love with him, but was terrified of facing him again. He stopped teasing her and treated her like a complete stranger but at times she caught him staring at her. It was Kanta who observed, "Karan doesn't seem to be happy anymore; he's too quiet. And I think Bimla is trying too hard to be with him." Krina had told Kanta of her love for Karan and herself had been wondering with jealousy why Bimla had been spending so much time with him.

After being busy appearing for the final exams, the last two weeks at school as per tradition were supposed to be fun with each house preparing to display their talent for the silver plaque, a performance that would be followed by a gala dinner. While everyone busied themselves with rehearsals, Krina was still upset at the way she and Karan treated each other like strangers.

On the night of the performance, Karan's team won with their dance. Krina admired his traditional Kinnauri dress: a knee-length woollen *kurti* with a pair of tight woollen trousers, *suthan*; a buttoned grey coat like an *achkan* called "*chuba*" with a frock-like flair below the waist; a sash, *kira,* around his waist called "*gachang*" worn over the *chuba*. The *suthan* which was woven with a multicoloured border up to the knees, was called "*topru*" or "*takoit suthan*", something worn only by the master artiste, not the entire troupe, though the rest of the costume was the same for all the other boys.

The girls wore a blanket like a *doru* draped from the left shoulder to the ankles over a full sleeve grey or black shirt with borders of red, orange or maroon lines. Their *cholis* were edged with velvet at the collar, cuffs and pockets. The famous Kinnauri shawl, *Kinnauri chhanli* in grey, black or cream with a woven border was folded double with the ends of the plain, middle portion pulled over the shoulders and pinned together at the breast with a brooch, leaving the patterned edges hanging over the sides and back. The boys and girls both wore a flat-topped cap called "*tepang*", and Iham footwear, made of untanned thin leather with knee-high felt uppers and *paiche* made of woven goat hair. The girls were adorned with necklaces of silver, turquoise and coral; matching earrings; silver rings, bangles and bracelets; and silver ornaments in their hair. All in all, it was an impressive sight.

She saw how happy her friend Bimla was standing next to Karan. She was always very confident with her willowy tall figure, sharp features, glowing white complexion and grey eyes. Her light-hearted jokes, flippancy and outgoing nature made her very popular with the boys. She was an only daughter of a senior army officer and at times became a little too selfish and determined to have her own way, which Krina and Kanta resented. Krina had wanted to be part of the team and perform the *Nati* dance, but Bimla told her that Karan had refused to let her join the team. She accepted this but could not resist attending the rehearsals, despite being told repeatedly by Bimla not to, where she watched Karan and admired his gracefulness as he danced and how well he could organise the team. She had fallen deeply in love with him. In the end, even Bimla became adept at the dance, and they won the plaque. The performance was appreciated greatly by the judges who declared it the most outstanding event of the year.

Dinner and a celebration followed the performance where Karan's friends once again thronged him holding the plaque. Krina was very quiet and did not congratulate him though she dearly wished to because she was afraid of being snubbed and humiliated in public. Without eating dinner she left the hall, but someone caught up with her.

"Krina." She turned around to see Karan. Holding the plaque he came close and said, "Please look at me; it's the last day of school." She looked at him shyly and began to blush as he came even closer and looked deep into her eyes. The music from the auditorium brought them back to the present. He placed the plaque in her hands and took her face in his own. "Won't you congratulate me?"

"Congratulations, you deserved it," she murmured.

He kissed her on the forehead. "Thank you, my Krina, but I want to tell you something…" He was cut off by the sound of footsteps. They saw a shadow move, as though someone left in a hurry. There followed a silence where Krina imagined the worst, and becoming frightened, handed the plaque back to Karan and ran off, leaving him calling out after her, "Wait, there's something I want to tell you!"

When she reached the house she could still see him standing where she'd left him and she was almost overcome by the urge to run back to him, but now Bimla was with him. She ran to her room and looked in the mirror. She could still feel the kiss on her forehead, and his words, "I want to tell you something," kept ringing in her ears. But the image of Bimla standing so close finally made her dissolve into tears. It was that night that she realised she would never love anyone else again.

This she confided in her father who perceived the delicacy of the situation and did not laugh. He patiently lent his ear to his beloved child but held her hand and said gently, "You're both too young to be in love; neither of you know anything about the real world outside your little protective shells. But I promise to keep this secret if you promise me that until your career is successfully established, you will not meet him, and neither will you be the first one to contact him. If he is still in love with you by that time, he will contact you himself. Promise me this and I will keep your secret and never ask you to get married till you're ready." Krina accepted and to date the secret remained only between father and daughter.

Kanta had been the one who told Krina that Karan had scored very low marks for the first time in his final exams. He left India to study medicine in Boston despite getting admission in a college in Delhi. She was tempted to contact him several times but did not break her promise to her father and the photograph she had of him became her only solace. Now as she lay holding the frame she recalled the beautiful American woman who called him "darling", how they looked at each other, how the woman blushed when he complimented her, and then for the first time resented her father for making her promise not to meet Karan, because now it was too late; he was a married man.

Tears welled up in her eyes and she lay holding the frame as she had done so many nights. In her heart she still knew that regardless of what Karan felt for her, she would love him forever. She placed a kiss on the photograph, held it to her chest, shut her eyes and succumbed to sleep.

# Chapter 3

A knock at the door awoke her at 7 am. The room was still warm from the fire in the grate and she snuggled deeper into her quilt, shutting out the nanny with her tea tray, who let in a cold draught and sunlight when she drew the curtains apart. "You said you wanted to visit the Hanuman temple today," she said, forcing Krina to sit up in bed. "It closes at 11 so you'd better get ready."

Sleepily Krina accepted the cup of hot tea and looked out of the window. She was once again greeted by the view of a clear sky and the valley bathed in sunlight. She drowned the last of her tea and got out of bed to get dressed in a grass green Pashmina Punjabi suit over a green skivvy, matching woollen cap and scarf, and walking shoes. She chose not to put any make-up on and pulled her hair into a simple ponytail. Ram Kumar, the driver, was already waiting for her and drove her to the bus stop and then up to Monkey Point, the highest point in Kasauli and the best place to see the sunset and view the plains from. From there they were allowed to visit the temple of Shri Baba Balak Nath which commands a 360 degree panoramic view and is adjacent to the Hanuman temple. Laying her head on the backseat of the car she closed her eyes. She must pray for the patience to forget Karan and her past. *I am free of my first love*, she told herself, but knew in her heart that she wasn't.

She left the car at Monkey Point and walked the narrow climb amongst the canopy of tall cedars. There weren't many people at that early hour, mostly women whom she supposed to be devotees of the Lord. She set out on a brisk pace and enjoyed the cool breeze from the north-east of the hills, the chirping of the birds and the tolling of the temple bells. A fifteen-minute climb later she saw the small temple with saffron flags. She remembered her mother saying that the temple is centuries old and that the Lord fulfils the wishes of every believer. Her father once brought her to this place at sunrise and again at sunset. It was a heavenly experience. The tolling of the bells was now almost continuous and being a staunch follower, she shut her eyes and prayed to Him to let her be free of her past so she could live her life the way she should, but stopped when she remembered that the previous night she couldn't even bring herself to tear Karan's picture; instead, she had slept clutching it to her chest.

She wept softly in the knowledge that in this life, she would never be rid of him. *Why am I so much in love with him that no one else attracts me?* In the morning while sipping tea her gaze fell on the photograph once again and immediately was drawn to his eyes and thought she would never love anyone else again. She hoped that praying to Hanumanji would show her the way. His cruel grip on her wrist the previous day and those large brown eyes staring at her brought tears to her eyes. *Why was he looking so intently at me?* She wondered for the hundredth time, but she still couldn't resolve it.

She was still deep in thought when she reached the temple where she took off her shoes and climbed the stairs after washing her hands. She bought a *thali* made of Pipal leaves with marigold flowers, incense, saffron *tilak*, a sweet and a *diya* for the prayer from a girl. The verandah of the temple was full of devotees standing in line holding their thalis, waiting for their turn. Krina covered her head with her scarf and took her place in line. Someone from behind said, "Since when did Krina become a devotee of Lord Hanumanji?"

She turned around at the sound of Karan's familiar voice. Taken completely off-guard by his presence, she forgot everything, even where she was, and the only thing that registered was how close he was standing to her. She smiled at him in his casual outfit, uncovered head and no thali and said, "Cover your head. Where is your thali? You must buy one to please the Lord!"

"Why?"

"I told you, to please him so he may grant you your wish."

"Well, no one's ever told me that in all the times that I came here."

"You've been visiting this temple?" she looked at him in surprise.

He looked at her seriously, "Yes, Krina. Every time I visit Kasauli since I finished school," but then he winked, "anyway, right now I have neither money nor something to cover my head with. Why don't you request Him to fulfil my wish for me?"

She laughed and told him to wait there. Giving him her own thali, she went down to buy another one. When she returned, he was no longer standing in line, but by the side of the upper stairs to the verandah in front of the temple. She whipped out her cap and put it on his head with a smile, but the smile vanished when he looked deep into her eyes. She couldn't look away, and neither of them knew how long they gazed at each other till the *panditji* interrupted them. There were no more devotees left and he was waiting for them. A deep flush crept to her face and she whispered to Karan to go first.

"No Krina, we will go and pray together today," he said seriously. Knowing how stubborn he was, she went with him. They placed their thalis together in front of the deity and lit the diyas and prayed with their eyes shut after the panditji recited the *shlokas*. He then put the saffron tilak on their foreheads and they bent to touch the feet of the deity. The panditji blessed them saying that they had the blessings of the Lord, and gave them *prashad*.

Karan turned to her and said, "Open your mouth." When she didn't he insisted, "Krina, just do as I say!" she opened her mouth and he put a piece of *prashad* in it. "Now don't just hold your *prashad*, do what I did. Don't argue, just do it." She put a piece in his mouth, too. "This is a ritual pandit Krina isn't aware of," he smiled that meaningful smile. "You know, *prashad* must be shared by two people who are close to each other. This is now the belief of Saint Karan." Krina turned away shy and restless but Karan gripped her shoulder. "Tell me what you asked for."

"Oh, Karan…"

His grip tightened. "Tell me."

"I asked for solace. What about you?"

"I thanked the Lord that after eight years I got what I wished for. I believed in him even as I followed my father's advice when I left for Boston."

Krina smiled. "I'm glad for you."

"Yes, this is the first time I'm happy and satisfied and have come to thank him with all my heart, though the true ritual was taught to me by my pandit Krina," he laughed.

All the other devotees had left and the temple closed so they turned to leave too. At the stairs, she said to him, "Can I ask you something? It's now seven years since we parted –"

"You're wrong. It's been eight years and seven days exactly. I counted each day."

"All right, if you've counted, eight years. Look, we're not kids any more," she looked at his eyes and a blush crept to her cheeks. He was silent and she waited for him to say something but his expression was so unreadable it made her nervous just as it had when they were in school. She continued, "Don't you think it's time we forgive and forget and become friends?"

"Do you want that?"

"Yes, Karan."

"If that's what you want, I want to see you happy. Let us be friends." She looked into his eyes once again and lost herself in them till his voice brought her back. "Look at me Krina." He took her hand and she felt her heart flutter. "I want to tell you something – "

"Karan! Darling where are you?" a woman's voice called.

Krina felt like she landed back in reality with a thud. She extracted her hand from his as her eyes misted over. "I'm sorry. You're very lucky. She's not only very beautiful but kind too, and I wish you two all the happiness you had asked the Lord for and he has granted you today." The sob in her throat didn't let her say more, so she pushed past him and ran down the stairs ignoring him calling after her, "Krina, please wait! I need to talk to you!"

Tears obscured her vision but she ran down the slope. How could she have been so foolish, living in a dreamland thinking the Lord had given her everything she had wished for? She climbed into her car and asked the driver to take her home, keeping her face hidden from view as she pretended to tie her shoelaces.

It was 10 am when she asked the driver to drive to School Rajanaika on the hill in north-east through the village of Gurkhal. As they drove down from the cottage she admired the scenic route along the forested mountain slope along the national highway from Dharmapur. At first it was dense with deodars and pines, but then the trees grew sparse because the law against cutting down of trees had been flouted by the rich who had build large bungalows to enjoy their retirement which gave them a view of the valleys, villages, streams and snow-covered peaks in the north-east. One of the palatial houses belonged to Karan's father, called "Thali House" where he kept stud horses for his son who had a passion for stallions. Karan often entertained his friends there and Bimla had told her that the house was furnished like a palace with an army of servants. Krina had listened eagerly but Kanta warned her not to say anything in front of Bimla who was now part of Karan's group and there was always a danger of their conversation being relayed to him.

The car slowed down at the village because it was no longer fit to drive through with its narrow roads encroached on by shops and herds of cattle running free without control. The car made its way very slowly out of the village, and she arrived at school somewhat late. There was no parking available, so she told the driver to wait in the car somewhere by the gate and started to get out of the car when she saw Karan escort the American woman into the school. She looked stunning in a woollen turquoise dress with matching heels and a shawl. Karan had been right when he'd said that blue suited her. Karan himself was dressed casually in grey. She knew how he hated to dress formally even for formal functions. "I thanked the Lord that after eight years I got what I wished for." His words rang in her ears. In an effort to avoid the couple she hid in the crowd of people entering the gate, and bumped into someone.

It was Kanta. "Krina!" she exclaimed. "I saw you and rushed right over to meet you! It's been so long." Krina hugged her back. "Come meet my husband, Ravinder. He's in the air force." They walked together hand-in-hand to the arena and found seats in the third row. Krina turned her head and saw Karan speaking to an army officer with the American woman close by.

Kanta introduced Krina and her husband who said, "We were in Dalhousie last year and had dinner with your parents at your house."

"How did you like Dalhousie?" Krina asked.

"It is beautiful. I see that the red tin roofs and chimneys from the days of the British Raj are still maintained. The best part of the town, though, is how it's shrouded in thick mist till midday."

"It seems you love mountains," smiled Krina.

"Yes, as do you, I've heard."

Kanta suddenly whispered to Krina, "Have you met Karan yet? Look, he's standing there," pointing at the couple now advancing "Yes, he has a beautiful wife."

Kanta looked bewildered. "What? He isn't married. That girl is Nancy Nelson from Boston.She is a staff nurse in Boston Hospital and had worked with Karan. She's like a sister to him. She's on a visit to India to see Thali and then will be on her way to Kinnaur and Tibet to write her book."

Now it was Krina's turn to be bewildered. "What?"

"What do you mean, 'what'? They aren't married. In fact, Ravi thought the same thing last evening when we bumped into them and Karan mentioned that he had been looking for a girl, and he was lucky to have finally found her. Don't you know which girl he's talking about?"

"Oh..."

"Don't miss this opportunity, Krina. I know you're still in love with him, and I'm sure he loves you too. Now look...he's going to take that seat behind us." Kanta sighed. "I envy you. How can a man love a woman so much that he is prepared to wait so long for her? If there is such a thing as true love, this is it. Oh, how I wish I was a writer!" she pinched Krina's arm. "You know, the two of you would have been together sooner had it not been for Bimla."

Krina became dizzy with barely contained glee. The shamiana in the sports ground where the function was being held became brighter as the sun shone through it. Karan was in love with her! *Oh God, that's what he wanted to tell me in the temple when Nancy called him and I ran away!* That was the second time he had been interrupted; he had probably wanted to say the same thing to her on the last day of school when she had left him outside the auditorium. She didn't even realise when a smile sprang up on her face till Kanta leaned over to whisper, "Don't turn around, but Karan is sitting behind you, and guess who's taken a seat behind him! It's Bimla with her boyfriend, Captain Bhulla. I guess she must have realised it's time for her to settle down, especially since she won't be getting any attention from Karan after the stunt she pulled."

"What are you talking about?"

"Last year she told Karan that you'd got married and moved to London. He was extremely sad when he met us at Shimla till I told him what happened on our visit to Dalhousie."

"What happened?"

"Well, after having dinner at your place, your father took us to see the beautiful view of the Dhaula Dhars from your room. There I saw the sketch Karan drew of the "langur" on the mantle above your fireplace. Your father told me no one was allowed to touch that sketch and then explained that you were still in love with Karan, that he had promised never to say anything to you till you decided to settle down, and that even your mother wasn't aware of it. When I told him that Karan was still looking for you and you two would soon be together, he blessed me. All this is what I told Karan at Shimla and he got terribly excited."

Someone tugged on Krina's scarf, and she turned around to see Karan holding out a note to her. It read in Karan's hand: *Krina, the tears I saw in your eyes told me Hanumanji had granted me what I spent eight years and now eight days praying for. He has blessed me.*

Though the note filled her with joy Krina decided not to look back and keep silent, knowing Karan would be longing to have her turn around. She knew he'd do something else to attract her attention and reply, so she waited patiently. Sure enough, there was another tug on her scarf and a note landed on her lap. This one read: *I think langurs wear the same light brown and black dress as yours, although you do look slightly better now.*

The function, delayed thus far because the chief guest was late, finally began. A hush fell over the audience as the Principal began the report about the school. He described the school's history and explained how to that day, the school had spread its 139 acres on an independent hill at a height of 5780 ft amidst a forest of pine and deodar. Then followed a talk by Major General Kumar about how old he felt when he thought of being a part of the school so long ago. His speech was well written and humorous as he spoke about mischief he and other well-known people used to get up to in school. The dean gave the vote of thanks and that was when Krina remembered that she had no idea how the dean had got hold of her new address. The audience was invited to have tea in the adjacent *shamiana* where she saw Karan talking to the dean. She wanted to be with him, but did not want to do so with Nancy around, so she told Kanta she was going back to her cottage and would see them all for the alumni dinner.

When she reached the gate, she looked around at the beauty of the afternoon in autumn. The mountainside was steeped in golden sunlight and it was a beautiful, clear day with no mist even at the mountaintop. The slope where she had first felt attracted to Karan beckoned her and she gave in to her love for the mountains. She slowly climbed up and was about to cross the road when someone pulled her back just as a car sped past almost running her over. "Be careful," said her rescuer, an army officer, "life is precious."

"Thank you!" she called out after him. She followed the side of the road to her favourite path up the slope. It was a narrow path flanked on both sides by tall trees. It was when the climb became a little more steep that she realised the path was wet with the mist from the morning and therefore slippery making it difficult to climb in her high heels. She took off her shoes and pulled on thick woollen socks so the thorns and pinecones wouldn't cut her feet. She reached the spot she spent so many hours at and looked at it affectionately. She breathed in the aroma of the pine needles in the breeze. The mist was very slowly rolling in at the top of the mountain but the sun's rays still cut through giving it a golden hue.

She sat down on the boulder and observed the people below. They were mostly sipping tea and chatting with one another, probably reminiscing about their school lives and their achievements since, catching up with old friends. She was happy in her solitude and it made her smile. Down the road the women carried bundles of wood on their heads climbing slowly and she was taken back to the time when Karan rode his stallion and tread close to the women to scare them. Karan the young boy she loved then and Karan the man she loved now. Yes, Kanta was right, this was true love. She couldn't wait to tell her parents whom she knew would accept it.

She thought she heard a soft voice call her name but when she looked around, she saw no one. She thought she must be dreaming but when she heard the voice repeatedly, there was no one. She chuckled thinking she was hallucinating in her joy so she shut her eyes and rested her head against a tree. She truly was blessed by Lord Hanuman today; she had got what she had also waited for all these years. She thought she felt a soft kiss on her cheek but when she opened her eyes, she only saw the mist that had slowly drifted down from the mountaintops. This time there was a very real, audible cough behind her and she turned around to see Bimla standing over her dressed in a deep green Punjabi suit. Of course Bimla knew this spot, as she had been Krina's close friend and once Krina had even brought her there. Krina did not mention anything to her about what had happened between her and Karan. Thinking of Karan reminded her of what Bimla had done to drive them apart and that infuriated her.

"Krina, what are you doing here?" Bimla asked innocently.

"Why?"

"Nothing, I'm just asking."

"I came here to enjoy the mountain air," was Krina's guarded reply.

"Oh, that's nice. How are you?"

"Fine, thank you."

"I waved at you but you didn't look at me."

"Oh. I'm sorry."

"So did you see Karan?" she asked somewhat anxiously.

"Was I supposed to?"

"I'm just asking! You seem changed."

Krina laughed. "Do I? How?"

Bimla came close. "Well, you're more mature and poised and look so beautiful and smart but you've become distant to friends like me."

"Really? I wonder why? I must not forget my old friends who were so close to me in school and always so concerned about my attachment to a boy named Karan."

"But…"

"No, no buts Bimla. Just let it be and keep me away from your gossip."

"All right. Let us go down and attend the dinner. I wish to go home and take some rest. I should go back to my fiancé who must be wondering where I've gone. You see I left quickly without telling him when I saw you trekking up."

"Well aren't you observant!" Krina turned around to leave. She bent down to pull her heels off for the trek back down, when suddenly she felt a push from behind. She would have lost her balance and gone tumbling down the mountainside but a firm hand caught her. Krina looked up to see Karan holding onto her with a very grim expression.

"I don't think I slipped. I think I was pushed!" she said to him.

"I know. Stay here." He hurried off down the path where Bimla was trying to make a quick getaway. Krina's heartbeat raced, she stood shaking where Karan had told her to stay. She watched Karan catch up to Bimla and grab her by the elbow. Bimla protested loudly as he dragged her back up to where Krina was standing after slapping her twice. The hard slaps left an impression on her face. Bimla looked pleadingly at Karan with frightened eyes begging him to stop. Krina realised she was not her friend, but a snake and Kanta was right when she told Krina to beware of her.

"Enough is enough," Karan threatened, "I do not have the patience to pardon you, so come out and tell the truth to Krina or not only will I have my guards beat you but I will also turn you over to the police for attempted murder!"

There was complete silence and then Bimla looked at Krina with blazing eyes. Thus far she had been shaking under Karan's grip but now she had regained her confidence and looked at them both with defiant eyes as Karan pulled Krina close. "Yes, I did push her because I hate her! I fell in love with you but you loved her and that made me so jealous! It was too much today when I saw you exchanging notes. I wanted to push her not to kill her but to deform her so the very sight of her would repulse you and you'd stop loving her!" She laughed a spiteful laugh that chilled Krina. "Do what you want, I don't care any more."

Bimla's fiancé suddenly came up behind her and caught hold of her when Bimla lost her balance and nearly fell. "Please," he said to Karan, "don't report her. I'll handle her." Still clasping her arm, he led her back down the slope carefully.

Krina and Karan watched them climb down and Karan said, "It seems that he really does love that wretch." Then holding her close, he said to her, "What a day! First Hanumanji blesses us and now this dreadful incident occurs. I'm lucky that I was here to save you, darling," and his hold tightened. "She was always there when I came for the Founder's Day function and used to talk with such feeling about you that I was convinced she was your faithful friend. It's

Kanta who exposed her and only then did I avoid her. I don't understand why she kept pursuing me despite knowing that the only person I love is you. I feel sorry for this man who's fallen in love with her and thinks he can change her ways." He held her face in his hands and looked deep into her eyes. "I fell in love with you under this bottle-brush tree and when you slapped me, I vowed that you're the only woman I'll ever have." He smiled and bent down to kiss her. They lost themselves in each other without a care for the world. Then Karan looked at her lovingly and said, "There's no mist, but a shine in your dreamy eyes, and now your lips will not let me leave you." The furious blush that covered Krina's face made her bend her head. Karan kissed her again but stopped and said regretfully, "I'm so sorry, but I must go. Nancy is very keen on meeting her cousin Paul in the cantonment club. We will be together again at eight tonight."

Looking at her shyness he laughed and took her hand. He led her carefully down the slope and after placing a kiss on her forehead whispered, "I love you. See you at eight."

# Chapter 4

It was exactly 8 pm when Krina reached the school and parked next to a white Benz. Its driver's side door opened and Karan stepped out dressed formally for once in a black suit and white silk shirt, looking extremely handsome. Her pulse quickened every time she saw him. Even though it had been so many years their love for each other had become firmly cemented. He went over to the passenger door and opened it for Nancy who looked stunning as usual with her shining blond hair, a long black gown and a turquoise shawl around her shoulders. Krina smiled. She knew turquoise was Karan's favourite colour. Nancy's gold jewellery and glass bangles shone in the light and Krina thought she looked even more graceful and beautiful in high heels and a matching handbag. Karan offered her his arm and escorted her to the venue. *Why wouldn't anyone think that they were a couple?* She wondered, this time without heartache.

She looked at her watch and thought she had time to visit the bottlebrush tree by the swimming pool where she'd had her first kiss, and she was keen to see Shivalik house as well. The air had a chill to it, but the unbounded joy she felt within her kept her from feeling the cold. There was complete silence by the pool as well as at the house; everyone was in the dining room. The tree looked as fresh and green as before, and the branches perhaps more lively as though dancing to the tune of the mountains carried by the wind. She stood under the tree thinking of her first kiss when she heard soft footsteps and a familiar scent of cologne wafted towards her.

Karan came up from behind and put his arms around her. "Karan," she whispered. He held her tighter and bent down to kiss her cheek.

"I knew my Krina will come here to remember our first kiss just as I did every year, thinking about the girl who never remembered me after leaving school."

"I wanted to, I even left my address with you but I had promised my father that I wouldn't try to contact you first. All I had to live on were your memories!"

Karan puller her closer still and said, "Krina, say those words I want to hear."

She looked into his eyes, "I love you. I have always loved you and you were, are and always will be the icon of my love forever."

He held her face in both hands and kissed her deeply and they shut out the whole world save each other but the sound of voices brought them back to the present. "Krina," he said with a smile, "Close your eyes. Today I am going to tell you what I've tried twice to say."

"What?"

"Please, Krina, there isn't much time, we have to return to the venue soon. Close your eyes." She did and felt a cold metal band being slipped onto the middle finger of her left hand. "Open your eyes!" She saw a simple gold ring on her finger, which he kissed. "This ring was given to me when I turned seventeen by my mother when I went to the temple Hath-Koti of Ma Bhawani's temple close to Rampur where my parents met and fell in love. There she gave me the ring and told me that I must respect and be honest to the woman I love and give this ring only to her when I decide to settle down. I have always cherished this ring and the thought of giving it to you. Now with this band we are bonded together forever, my love, and you must never take it off without my permission or I shall be very cruel and cut off your finger. You know how much I have suffered in waiting for you, for this day."

She nodded and kissed him. The sound of music made them reluctantly pull away and Karan said with a smile, "I don't ever want to break this embrace, but we must get back to dinner." He nearly dragged her back to the auditorium.

When they arrived they discovered everyone taking their places at their tables so the dinner could begin because they still abided by the principles their school had taught them, one of which was to value time. Karan held Krina's hand and told her, "You will be at the same table as me, right before my eyes so I can reassure myself that this isn't just a dream." The two of them strode into the auditorium together.

The tables inside were arranged only for two people each, with red tablecloths and candles in the centre. Almost all the tables were occupied but Karan spotted an empty table by the stage. There were whispers and smiles all around as those who knew Karan saw the two walk in together. Shyly she tried to extract her hand from his, but his grip was too tight. Dean Varma and Nancy were standing close to the table, and Krina was formally introduced to the dean and Nancy. But Nancy ignored Krina and demanded of Karan, "Where were you? Everyone was asking about you!"

He turned to Krina and said, "Krina, Nancy worked as the staff nurse at my theatre and was interested in visiting India. She wants to write a book – nothing like your poems, of course – about the high mountains of Kinnaur and Tibet before she returns to Boston."

Nancy turned to Krina and said with a smile, "We have met, and now I understand why Karan was so rude even though he knew you were not a salesgirl in that shop."

'Oh, well, you know Karan," laughed Krina.

The audience became silent as the dean came on stage. He talked about the enthusiasm, the togetherness and the respect the alumni still had for the school that touched him, but then he held up a hand and said that he didn't want to make his speech too long lest certain members of the audience began pelting him off the stage with anything they could get their hands on so dinner could commence. Everyone laughed. "I know that we come, meet and relive the past on this same day every year. Let us enjoy this year, too, and now I will leave the stage so this year's entertainment, dinner and drinks can begin. All I would like to say to you in the end is our school motto: Never relent – Fight for honour. I hope to see you all back here next time as well."

The audience applauded and another man, dressed in a woollen beige kurta, light churidar pajama and kulu topi, took the microphone and said, "Today as I look around it makes me wonder what this school has given you that you all love it so intimately. It reminds me of something someone once said, 'Is it a place where you feel near the celestial bodies, where the sun and the moon are your neighbours and the stars your friends? But above all, the growing years of pain, sorrow and happiness under the third eye who wishes you to become something in life has bound you to respect this temple of learning.'" The audience applauded. "Now, coming back to the agenda for tonight, I am responsible for the entertainment and my channel has prepared a few items for you that we will record and later broadcast.'

Krina recognised the gentleman. It was Mr Sidharth Sharma, the director of a local television channel in Shimla whom she had met by chance while giving an audition of the song 'Chanchlo' a week ago. She turned to tell Karan but stopped when she realised that he had only been staring at her all the while and out of the corner of her eye she noticed that Nancy was looking at Karan very closely, too. He touched his left cheek and Krina was reminded of their kiss, which made her blush deeply.

The director announced the performance of the Gaddi dance by local artistes and the house lights were dimmed. They played local *Pahari* instruments like drums, pipes, the flute, conch shells and bells to which danced a troupe of men and women in typical Gaddi dresses of *chola*, *dora*, and *chauli topi* on their heads. Their dress and jewellery reminded her of the time she was in Bharmaur with her family and her grandfather had insisted she join the dancers. The song, *'Lal tera Safa Bhora, Bhore teri Kalgi ho, Bohre teri Kalgi Bhora, Bani Bani Pandi ho,'* began playing and the dancers' feet moved in perfect unison, completely capturing the audience.

It was followed by a recitation by one of the students from Krina's and Karan's own batch, Mohamad Sadiqui, who even at school was always lost in his own musings on philosophy and often recited Ghalib's couplets. Karan looked at Krina and winked because he knew they were both thinking the same thing: they used to sit quite close by to each other in the school's dining hall and sometimes Mohamad used to recite his compositions. Karan never enjoyed that and Bimla once told her that he used to say, "That man is a mad philosopher just like your dull, ugly, asocial friend, Krina." Krina had been hurt but decided not to care.

She was so lost in her thoughts that she didn't even notice when Mohamad got off the stage and the audience applauded. The house lights came on and the drinks were served. However, there was an announcement, "Although I have not taken permission from the lady in question, I am sure she will oblige us with a folk song. You all know her though she sings under a pseudonym." As the director looked at their table, Krina knew it was her he was talking about. "Ladies and gentlemen, please give a round of applause for Ms Karuna Singh!"

Krina went onstage and introduced the song she was about to sing. "The people of Himachal Pradesh are simple, hard working and helpful, and they live in close-knit communities. On major occasions like Dussehra in Kullu, Shivratri Lavi and Minjar in Chamba, the festivities continue through village fairs where they compose songs to which they dance accompanied by a simple orchestra of local instruments. The song 'Neelama' was composed by famous singers of the land. It's a simple romantic song sung by a young Gaddi man in praise of a beautiful shepherdess who has taken her sheep out to graze." She nodded at the small orchestra behind her and two girls on either side of her fell into step as Krina began singing the song and dancing.

*"Bhedha Terian Ho.Ho*
*Chugdia Bhatni Neelama.*

*(1)* *Biteh Nalua Ho. Ho.*
*Mera boho gharat Neelama.*
*Girls-Bhedha Terian Ho. Ho.*
*Biteh Nalua ho ho*
*(2)* *Main gunvan ho ho*
*Too sogi sogi ganvan Neelama*
*Tun ganvan ho ho.*
*Main Bansari bajawan Neelama.*
*Girls-Bhedha terian Ho Ho.*
*Bitch Nalua Ho Ho..*
3. *Galan terian Ho Ho...*
*Mithari Makhir Neelama.*
*Main tan padni ho. ho.*
*Teri naina di kitab Neelama*
*Girl-Bhedhan terian ho ho.*
*Bitch Nalua ho ho.*
4. *Phul Khiria ho. ho.*
*Khilia Gulab Neelama.*
*Tu-tan lagdi Ho ho.*
*Ranjuan di heer Neelama.*
*Bhedhan terian ho ho.*
*Chughdia bhatni Neelama.*
*Bitch Nalua ho ho.*
*Mera bho gharat Neelama.*
5. *Panechi uddhe ho ho.*
*Lambia udhan Neelama.*
*Do dil mildhe ho ho.*
*Jaldha Jamana Neelama.*
*Girls-Bhedha terian Ho Ho.*
*Chugdhia bhatni Neelama*
*Bitch Nalua Ho. Ho.*
*Mera bho ghoral Neelama.*

The audience loved her performance and demanded an encore

but Krina politely refused, handing the mike back to the director and returning to her table. As she was sitting down, Nancy touched her arm and said, "I didn't follow the words but that melodious voice, your graceful dance, and that lovely tribal dress of yours were just enchanting. Karan," she continued, "won't you get me that dress on our way to Thali?"

He was quiet as the plates were set at the table, and finally Karan replied, first taking Krina's hand in his own, "Nancy, you must know the truth. We are friends and I never crossed any limits with you, and you already knew this about me in Boston; everyone there wondered why every year around this time I return to India. To a certain extent it was because of my love for my school, but also because this is where I vowed that if Karan settles down with a woman, it would be Krina. I finally found her after eight years and seven days. Our elders felt we were too young to understand love, but they promised to wait and see if our love was true. I was separated from Krina and sent to Boston, but I never forgot my first love. This year I was asked to return from Boston and you came with me. At first when we arrived here, my mother thought that we'd got married, but then my father told me that Krina was here and that I must meet her because he had learnt from her father that she was still in love with me. I had never been happier. In the shop I wanted to take her into my arms but hurt her instead because I thought that she had made no effort to look for me when I had suffered all along, though now I know the truth. I got everything I wished for in the temple. Nancy, I love her so much that even if I had been forced to marry someone else, I would never have stopped loving her."

Nancy smiled and said, "That day in the shop I wondered about her. I wasn't so much of a fool to be blind to what was going on between you two. That day you seemed restless, very different from how you used to behave in Boston. Everyone there thought that you had no interest in women, but no one knew why." She turned to Krina. "You will be the envy of so many women who strive for such love and devotion. I know why he loves you. It's because you're so different." The coffee was served and then Nancy added, "I'll be leaving soon, but I hope the two of you will always consider me a friend and see me if you ever visit Boston."

"We will, Nancy," Karan said, "but for now we will stay here to make up for all the time we've lost. And then there's our wedding, of course. Father wants us to be married in days rather than weeks." He winked at her. "Now don't tell me you want to wear the tribal dress Krina has on at the wedding." Nancy laughed at that.

It was late when they left the school but Karan told Krina to meet him on the hill above the television tower at 9.30 the next morning. "Think of me before going to sleep tonight," she whispered to him. "You know I'll be thinking of you." With a kiss on her cheek, he left.

She did think of Karan but got no sleep that night; she was far too excited by the events of the day. She held his photograph again and thought about him. She didn't know him before she was shifted to Shivalik house in the final term though she had not failed to notice him. All she knew then was that he was the ex-royal prince of the State of Thali and had a palatial house close to the school with an entire army of guards and servants, especially to attend to his stud horses. He was known to entertain his friends at his house on weekends. The first time she actually came into contact with him was when she, Bimla and Kanta were moved from their house to Shivalik. They left their luggage in the waiting area for the servant to take up to their rooms when Karan and his friends entered and asked the girls to introduce themselves. The other two introduced themselves as "Kanta Sharma" and "Bimla Kapoor" but Krina simply gave him her first name.

"Oh, look, she's trying to be mysterious and hide her surname." Karan and his friends laughed cruelly.

Krina grabbed Kanta's hand and said, "Let's go," even though Kanta warned her that she was being rude and that Karan did not tolerate insults and would make her life miserable.

"Look, what a baby, she needs someone to support her while she walks!" Karan jeered.

At the time Krina hadn't cared but that evening the three of them were ostracised in the dining room. This became routine, and though Kanta always stayed by Krina's side, Bimla immediately changed sides and expressed her wish to become friends with Karan.

One day when Krina was playing tennis, Karan entered the court and asked her to play against him. His friends were standing around them, and she knew he was going to try to humiliate her in front of them. She refused to reply, so he warned, "Play or I'll make you!" Completely alone and without the support of her own friends, Krina grew frightened and began to play. Though Krina was a skilled tennis player, Karan was better and gave her a tough time, making her run all over the court. At the end, she lost and he came over to ask, "Your name, madam?" But he cut her off before she could reply and said, "Oh, I'm sorry, I have no wish to know a first name without the surname. Don't ever underestimate Karan Singh."

His friends hooted and clapped as they left Krina almost in tears. That was when she realised that she had to be careful of him in the future. Back in her room, though, something nagged at her. How had he found out that she played tennis? She had never talked openly about it. She was sure someone had told him to provoke him into a confrontation with her. They did not talk to each other but sometimes after that day she caught him staring at her with an unreadable expression.

The next week he came up to her in the dining hall and said, "I've heard you think you're good at horse riding! Since it's Sunday tomorrow, you will ride with me tomorrow morning down to Dharampur."

Krina refused. "I don't know how to ride."

"Good, then I'll teach you." His authoritative voice coupled with the expectant stares of all his admirers frightened her into agreeing.

"7 o'clock at the gate. Don't be late."

Krina was convinced now that someone was feeding Karan information on her. Kanta suggested that it might be Bimla and told Krina to be careful of what she said to her.

At 7 the next morning Karan who was at the gate accompanied by two grooms was holding a whip waiting for her. "Ram Dev, help her onto Babar," he instructed.

Ignoring his instruction, she went to the horse and stroked his nuzzle while she murmured soothingly in his ear. She didn't notice when Karan came over to stand next to her, observing what she was doing. When she realised he was next to her, she took the whip from Ram Dev and said, "Thank you, but I can mount by myself." She hoisted herself onto the saddle and asked Karan who looked surprised, "Where to?" But he made no reply, only trotted off. She leaned close to Babar's ear and said, "Let's gallop." She whipped the horse gently and he shot forward, overtaking Karan.

It had been such a long time since she had ridden that it was a while before she wanted to slow down or even noticed that Karan was riding alongside her.

"Let's turn around. I say, the person who told me you were good at riding was right." They stopped their horses and he said, "Can we be friends?" he offered his hand.

Krina was still furious with him for insulting her and rode on ahead without replying. She knew she was already treading on thin ice and had probably provoked him even more by ignoring him but her fury was refuelled when she saw his crowd of admirers – among whom was Bimla – cheering and waiting for him at the gate. She was so upset she dismounted and ran up to her room to cry. Once again, Karan and she did not speak to each other.

One day during a morning walk she looked at the clear sky and slight mist around the mountains called out to her. She trekked up the slope that grew to be her favourite and found the boulder next to the pine tree. She could see the road below where women were zigzagging across the road because someone mounted on a horse was chasing after them. She looked closer and saw that it was

Karan. The sight made her chuckle and it was the first time she realised that she might have feelings for him. From that day on, she would rise early and trek up to the boulder with her camera and diary where she clicked pictures of the mountainside and composed poems.

One day she saw him coming down the slope and spontaneously clicked a picture of him, and had no idea at the time that he had seen her. About a week later she heard the sound of hooves and turned around to see Karan leading his horse to where she was sitting. Scared, she collected her diary and camera and ran back down the path but slipped and fell on some wet pine leaves. Karan laughed when he caught up with her. Irritated, she stuck her tongue out and gestured at him like a langur. It was from that day that he began calling her 'pahari langur'.

Only when she reached her room did she realise that she had dropped her diary in her panic. She went to look for it in the evening but when she didn't find it she was sure Karan had taken it. Her cheeks burned as she thought of him going through her personal diary, reading every private thought she'd had and every poem she'd written. She couldn't even ask for it back.

From that day he never let go of an opportunity to call her a Pahari langur and tease her in front of his friends. One day he slipped a piece of paper into her pocket. She opened it to find a sketch of a langur sitting on the boulder under the tree. It was signed, 'Karan'.

The constant teasing didn't let up; he would sit in front of her in the dining hall, take a bite of his food and then drop it on her plate, daring her to eat it. If she didn't, she knew he would tell everyone about the contents of her diary. She also hoped that if she did as he said, he would return it to her. Kanta warned her not to say anything in front of Bimla whom the two now suspected was relaying everything to Karan.

She had no place to hide; wherever she went, he was there: The temple of Goddess Kali and of Lord Krishna, the Gothic style small chapel with stained glass windows, the Shivaji hall which hosted plays, shows, films and lectures, the solar heated indoor swimming pool, indoor sports complex, squash court, firing range and gymnasium.

Somehow her feelings for him grew fonder despite the teasing but he never invited her to his house even on his birthday. Krina realised bitterly that he had no interest in her other than making a spectacle of her. She decided not to visit the hill for some time and tried to avoid eating at the dining hall when he was there. However, he seemed to be making a greater effort to be present whenever Krina took her meals, be it early morning or late night. He would take a seat near her and stare at her. The teasing became unbearable because his friends were always there, laughing.

She often thought of confronting him but didn't have the courage to, not while he had her diary. So the teasing continued and her feelings grew and it all led to that day under the bottlebrush tree...

Still clutching the photograph, Krina slowly drifted into sleep.

# Chapter 5

Krina left for her rendezvous a little past 9.30 the following morning. She wondered why he wanted to meet her at the hill above the television tower because she had believed that it was her special place and no one else knew about it. The sun offered no warmth and the morning was chilly, making her glad she had pulled on a skivvy and a woollen cap. She reached the top of the hill and relished the scent of pine in the air. From the top she could see the grassy valley of Solan and knew Chandigarh lay beyond the rugged Shivalik hills. Soon it would become her home for the winter because her mother's health didn't allow her to be too far from her doctors' care at PCIMER. She was glad to be going to Chandigarh though she was going to miss her hometown, Dalhousie, 7500ft above sea level, surrounded by the snow-capped Dhauladhar range, shrouded with thick mist, with Kala-top and Dain-kund nearby.

She turned the other way to look at the Sutlej winding like a serpent around the mountains but she was surprised to see that something had changed on the hill. Uncle Paul's cottage was gone. In its stead stood a white two-storeyed mansion with a red-tiled roof and huge lawns. She could see two cars parked at the porch and what looked like two guards stationed outside. In all probability Uncle Paul had sold his cottage to someone wealthy.

Sighing, she went to the boulder and looked at the pine tree where her father had engraved her name with a knife and was very pleasantly surprised to see that Karan had engraved his own name next to hers. Now she knew why Karan had wanted her to meet her there.

She flipped open her sketchbook and began to sketch when she thought she heard the sound of hooves and then someone snatched the book out of her hand. "Karan!" she exclaimed, "You're late." He made no reply, merely sat down next to her and began to modify her sketch. She looked at him while he worked on a figure of a monkey and finally said, "What? There's no monkey sitting here!"

"Then what's this sitting next to me?" he winked and pulled her into his lap.

"You're late," Krina accused.

"No I'm not," he jerked his thumb at the tree. "I was right here, carving my name, wondering why I'm so in love with this Dalhousie Langur." Krina pushed him away in mock-anger but he said seriously, "Look, we've both proved to our parents that true love does exist and is unaffected by even distance and time. You know, the day school ended, I wept. My father said to me that royal blood never weeps when I told him that that day I had lost the girl I loved." He looked at the tree trunk. "But now soon we will be husband and wife."

"By the way, how did you find out about this place?" she asked.

"We have so much to catch up on, how I found this place we'll discuss later. Come let's go to my place for lunch." He clasped her hand and said, "Now don't say a word till I tell you to." She quietly nodded as he led her down the hill to the road canopied by deodars. After a short walk they reached a house with beautiful bougainvillea growing along its boundary wall. He stopped outside the gate and smiled at her. "Surprise! This is our new home."

"Karan!" she gasped.

"It was a surprise to me too when this year my parents asked me to come back in September just after I got registered as a general surgeon-cum-organ transplant specialist in Boston. They had sold our old house in Kasauli and bought this new one for me." They continued down the road and he pointed out the beautiful terrace gardens just below the road and the trees laden with fruit and a small lookout hut with a thatched roof. The idea of living with such a picturesque view filled her with joy. "Come," he said and they entered the gate together and walked past the sprawling lawns on either side, up to the wide marble steps that led to the house, which looked like a diamond on a green carpet of grass. "Welcome to the house of two Ks, of Karan and Krina," he said to her. She looked up to see the words 'Ashiana of the two Ks' carved above the doorway.

There was a host of guards behind them and eyes from every window of the house looking at the couple, anxious to catch a glimpse of the bride-to-be. The heavy door with gold latches swung open and a tall woman in her mid-fifties wearing a Kinnaur tribal dress appeared holding a silver thali laden with a bowl of oil, marigold flowers, a diya and pieces of *burfi.* She poured the oil at the entrance and after throwing the marigold petals on the couple, put tikas on both their foreheads, told Krina to first take a bite of the burfi, the rest of which she put in Karan's mouth and blessed them both. Karan laughed but Krina bent down to touch her feet and when she looked up she saw tears in the woman's eyes.

"Krina, meet my nanny, Taruna Devi. She brought me up to this age." He turned to his nanny, "Now am I allowed to bring her inside?"

His nanny laughed and told Krina, "He is haughty and difficult to control, but I'm sure you'll do a fine job." She stepped back to let them enter.

The passageway between the two halves of the house was carpeted, chandeliers hung from the ceiling and huge portraits of Karan's ancestors in gold and silver frames hung on both walls. Karan opened the third door on the left and they entered a hall with a carpeted oak staircase that led up to the first floor. The hall itself was spacious and bathed in sunlight that streamed through the open bay windows. She looked up at the roof that was intricately carved and had crystal chandeliers suspended from it. She walked over to the central bay window where the heavy red velvet curtains bordered with lace had been drawn apart, allowing an unobstructed view of the rolling hills, the dense forests, and the valleys, and the nature so alive.

The room was furnished according to the taste of royalty in reds, and greens, with carved furniture made of dark oak. Above the fireplace hung a portrait of Karan in his princely robes sitting on a throne with the insignia of the sun behind it. Karan put his arms around her and said, "Even though the man you're looking at will be with you forever, I'm going to leave you for a while because I'm famished!" he left her to her musings as she walked out to a covered balcony and saw the view she had been trying to see clearly since she'd reached the house, that of the Dhaula-Dhars. She took a seat on the sofa and completely lost herself in her surroundings. A man in a white uniform appeared with a tea tray. Apart from the cups, which were china, everything including the tray was made of silver. *The royals really know how to live. This entire set must be so expensive.* She remembered how while at school Karan had entertained his friends without giving a single thought to money. Krina had heard about lavish parties hosted at his Kasauli house from Bimla who had also once expressed the desire of being a prince's wife. The door opened once again and Karan strode in. "Two cubes for Krina," he instructed.

"How did you know?" she asked.

"From watching you," he smiled. "My langur was seen very often consuming cookies and tea at the Gupta stores." He leaned against the balcony railing and said to her, "Now tell me everything that happened since the day I kissed you and you slapped me."

She laughed and replied, "Your slap was so hard and it was very cruel of you to push me."

"Now don't repeat that; I'm waiting for the rest of the story."

"Today it is eight years and nine days since then." She sipped her tea quietly.

"Did you ever think of calling me these eight years? Krina, please, I wish to hear everything before I lose my patience!"

She set her cup down. "All right, yes I did. I thought of you every day at Delhi and then even in Australia and Edinburgh. That photograph of you on your stallion was always by my side and often when I missed you too much, I would hold it and sleep. My father caught me one day when he walked in on me holding it. We had a long talk that day. He told me that he'd wait for you and if you came back to me we'd be married, but he would never force anything on me. Neither did he mention it again nor did he say anything to my mother. When I was leaving to go abroad, he told me to hold onto my love because it was so strong that he was sure you would return."

Karan came close and took the cup from her hands. "I was just as much in love with you as you were with me, but I was so angry with you for forgetting me that I used to curse you for never contacting me."

Krina trembled under his touch. "When I was in England, I often had the urge to call you, but I had made a promise to my father."

Someone came in to tell them that lunch would be ready in half an hour.

Karan clutched her hand and said, "Go on, Krina, I need to hear your story before I can tell you mine."

"All right. When you kissed me, I slapped you but when I looked into your eyes, I knew I was in love, but before I could say anything, you slapped me back and threw me on the ground." She covered her face with her hands and he gently removed them.

"That face haunted me every day in Boston. I always wondered what happened that night after I left."

"I couldn't swim," she continued, "my elbow was bleeding, so I went to the first aid room to get it bandaged, and then to the dining room to see you. I waited for you but you didn't come. I refused to eat too and madam Sharma forced me to have a glass of milk because otherwise I would get hunger cramps at night. I waited till everyone left but you still didn't come. I thought of going to your room but I was too scared. I didn't get any sleep that night so I decided to meet you the next morning when you would return from your daily ride. So I got up early and went outside, but Bimla stopped me and told me that you'd bet your friends that you could kiss me and that I was a fool for trying to come to see you. I was so horrified I ran all the way back to my room but on the way I stopped to look back and saw Bimla talking to you. I wondered then whether she was your friend or mine. From that day onwards I was really sad because you stopped talking to me altogether and Kanta commented on how you had become suddenly very quiet."

"She noticed that? Yes, I was so depressed I couldn't even study because you were always on my mind."

"Those were tough days for me, even though our schedules had become so hectic with the exams coming closer. After the exams, when the inter-house competition was held where you performed the nati dance, I asked Bimla if I could join the team, but she said that you had told her not to let me. I was heartbroken but I couldn't resist coming to watch you at rehearsals. Then when you won the plaque you called me outside and kissed my forehead, it was such a pleasant surprise! You were going to tell me something but then there were those footsteps…"

"Krina, I was so excited that night. I was going to tell you I loved you and give you the ring till Bimla showed up. I was so angry I left."

"The next morning I was going to leave very early with my parents so I wrote a letter to you confessing my love and left my address and phone number for you to call me. You weren't in your room yet so I slipped it under your door. The next morning I was confident I would hear from you, but while I was leaving I saw you going to the car park. My father asked the driver to wait for you, but you never came. My only hope was the letter I left for you, the picture of you I had clicked, the sketch of the langur you made, and the memory of the kiss when you had given me the plaque. Our trip to Dalhousie was delayed by a day and I waited for you at the cottage but you never called. Then the years passed and you still didn't call. I grew slowly to resent you too."

He hugged her tightly and wiped the tears from her eyes before saying, "Let's go inside now. I'm hungry." Hand-in-hand they entered a beautiful pink and white dining hall, which also had bay windows that boasted a view of the Dhaula-Dhars. His suite was furnished to his taste; everything was blue, red and white. "This is our suite," he said, "we'll both start visiting this house often now." He led her out to another balcony and seated her on the sofa there. "Go on, I'm waiting. What happened next?"

"Oh, well, I went to Delhi to study where I worked very hard to get you off my mind. My anatomy and physiology partners, Thakur Rajinder Singh (the only son of the ex-royal Raja Gulab Singh of Ram Garh, Uttrakhand) and Chander-Kumar Varma (the only son of a rich business man from Dehra Dun) and I became such good friends that we were known as the Three Musketeers in college and our motto was 'all for one, and one for all'. Rajinder was a fun-loving person and also fond of riding like me, so every Sunday we went to the polo club. He was very good at polo and I found him very interesting."

"Oh? And how was he?"

"What do you mean?"

"To look at."

At first Krina didn't reply but Karan glared at her. "He looked regal. Must have been six feet or maybe more and he had an athletic body like yours. He was very fair with sharp features and had black eyes. He lived in Rampur house till during the fourth term it was compulsory for him to stay in the hostel, but despite his wealth he was very modest." She paused to look at Karan before continuing with a smile. "We were friends because we had common interests, but I was not in the least attracted to him."

Karan was silent but finally said, "And what about Chander?"

She laughed. "He was a philosopher, tall and a gentleman like Rajinder but not as good looking. He used to compose poetry and even came on air on the radio several times. It was he who introduced me to some local radio and TV channels. It's thanks to him that I became Karuna Singh the budding folk singer. He hated medicine and quit in the final year to join the IAS, for which he trained in Mussoorie where fell in love with a girl and married her. Now he's a secretary in some Ministry at Delhi. He did have feelings for me, though. He found out I had a fondness for dark chocolate and now every birthday he sends me a card and chocolates."

"Oh."

"However, it was Rajinder who asked for my hand. His father approached mine and Rajinder proposed to me when I returned from Australia. Of course, I refused him, but he was so much in love with me that he said he would not stop asking me to marry him till I did get married – to him or someone else," she laughed, "but he remains a good friend and nothing more. Now when I was in Australia doing my pre-examination course, I had a friend called Margaret Rice who was half French and half Australian. Her cousin Peter fell in love with me but I told him firmly that the only man I would ever love was Karan. Soon after, I got a fellowship in England," her eyes twinkled. "You know, Margaret tells me that Peter still hasn't married."

He waited. "Anything else?"

"Yes."

"What now?"

"I love you!" Krina laughed.

"Oh do you?"

"Yes, I do. I told my parents that if you didn't marry me, I'd become a monk! Can you imagine me in a monk's guise?"

He took her back inside and they took a seat before the fireplace that was now lit. "Krina," he said placing a kiss on her forehead and then stroking her hair, "when I saw you in that shop I was so excited I wanted to take you in my arms, but then I remembered how much you had hurt me, so I decided to hurt you too. I flirted with Nancy to make you jealous and she thought I was falling for her. However, when I explained to her that we are in love, she decided to go back to Boston and was no longer interested in visiting the Himalayas.

"You see, I'm an only child and I was spoiled by my grandparents when I was young. It was for that reason that my father decided against sending me to Bishop Cotton School, which he had attended, and sent me here to Kasauli, instead. It took me a while to adjust, but slowly I got used to living with the so-called commoners of my state. My father always said that it was easy to buy friends but the true test was becoming a hero and being admired by them. Those words pushed me to excel in not only studies but in sports and every other field as well, but I still remained proud of my royal heritage and also quick-tempered. I was the prefect of my house and used to dominating everyone else, so when three girls moved in and one of them refused to tell us her surname, it really bothered me. We had come to welcome you, but you left abruptly and then Bimla told us that you were rude and snobbish. She said that she had known you a long time but that time you'd gone too far, so we decided to teach you a lesson. We all shunned you, but you kept up your reserved attitude, looking unperturbed by what was going on, seemingly content with just Kanta and Bimla.

"Then one day Bimla told us that you considered yourself to be very good at writing poetry, horse riding and tennis. So I went to the tennis court to teach you another lesson. I beat you at the game, but I inwardly did admit that you were a competent player. Then one day I tried to make amends and talk to you, but you refused to say a single word to me. So, to egg you on further, I said at the dining table so everyone could hear that since you didn't have a surname you probably came from an orphanage! Oh, you should have seen your eyes that day. You looked like you would murder me! Then there was the horse riding incident – believe me, it was Bimla who provoked me to do all these things – after which I genuinely respected you and began to have feelings for you, but then I also knew your fear of my threats. Do you remember that day in the swimming pool when I held your leg and frightened you? You didn't come to swim for weeks after that!" he laughed. She stirred but he said, "No, wait, let me finish. One day while horse riding my horse missed a step because of the flash from your camera. I saw you sitting up on your boulder and decided to frighten you even more. So about a week later, I crept up behind you and that's when you dropped your diary. I loved reading it, and I swear I never showed it to anyone. The more I read what you'd written, the more I liked you. You became my obsession and I began following you around. Poor Krina, you were so scared of me but little did you know that

Karan had fallen for someone so simple but so different from everyone else.

"Then that day when I saw you walking to the swimming pool, I decided I had to tell you how I felt so I caught up with you and kissed you. Even though you slapped me, I was elated because I'd seen the look in your eyes when I pushed you and I knew you loved me too. I couldn't sleep that night so I wrote a long letter to you saying how much I loved you and wished to marry you. I gave it to Bimla to give to you the next day before my morning ride, but she brought it right back saying you had ripped it into small pieces and insulted me. I was furious with you and at breakfast asked Kanta where you were, and that's when I began to doubt Bimala. Kanta told me that you had left early that morning for Chandigarh to see your mother who was in the hospital. I wondered whether Bimala could have given you the letter before you left, and now I know she didn't. I tried to catch you later to talk to you but you never let me, and soon there was no time because the exams were approaching. After the exams when we began rehearsing for the dance, I told my friend Pradeep to tell ask you to join us, but he told me that you had refused. I was hurt and confused when I saw you sitting and watching us practise. The day of the performance Pradeep confessed that Bimla had made him lie. I tried talking to you that night but Bimla showed up again. I never received the letter you say you left though when you mentioned it, I did remember Bimla being in my room and picking something up but at the time I thought nothing of it. After everything that had happened, she told me that she was in love with me. That night I broke my royal code and slapped her, and literally threw her out of my room. The next morning I went to find Kanta to ask where you were, but she said you had already left. I went to the car park but I didn't see you there, so I assumed you really had left. I was very angry with you for leaving without even trying to contact me. But now it's all over; we're finally together." He looked at Krina and realised she had fallen asleep with her head on his shoulder. He smiled fondly and lay her down on the sofa.

It was late evening when she finally woke up. Embarrassed at having fallen asleep she blushed till she saw Karan sitting next to her holding her diary. "Hey, this is mine! Give it to me!"

"I won't!" he pulled it out of her reach. "It's really helped me. Because I had this diary, you did everything I asked."

"I did everything you asked because I was afraid you'd tell everyone everything that I had written and make fun of me in front of your friends."

"But I didn't."

"I know. Why, though?"

"Because of this. Listen," he opened the diary and read out, "*Through the narrow break in the leaves I saw the road. Somehow this young man, so tall and handsome with windblown hair came riding down majestically on his black stallion. He made me look more and more at him until slowly I began falling for him. I brought my camera and instead of taking pictures of the hills, I took a picture of him. I am I in love with him?*"

"Stop!" Krina flushed.

"Now listen to what I wrote: *I couldn't control myself. I went down to the bottlebrush tree and stood behind her. I held her and kissed her, forgetting everything except that she was mine. I was very sad the day I left school and when I cried my father told me the first royal quality was of having the ability to control one's emotions. If you ever weep, you must weep alone. Then he laughed and said that if it was true love, he would help me and she would be his daughter-in-law someday.*" He looked at Krina with serious eyes. "My father asked for your address but all I knew was that your surname was Khanna, though I think now that my guard, Ram Singh knew where you lived and must have told him. My father then told me how he had a similar experience with my mother but he won her in the end because of the strength of his love and his determination to have her as his wife. Like your father, mine too said he would never force me to marry till I decided to. He said the following day he would take me to meet someone if my love were true and if I had faith. That night I re-read your diary and that page where you wrote that you were falling in love with me, and it gave me hope. He took me to the Hanuman temple for the first time where I promised Him that if you returned my love and came back to me someday, I would be His devoted follower. So Karan the atheist became religious for Krina. I was ready to start medical school in Delhi but my father sent me to Boston instead, but every year I would come to Kasauli in the hope of seeing you at the Founder's Day and also to visit the temple, and I never needed Hanumanji more than I did last year when Bimla told me that you had got married in London. But then I ran into Kanta who told me that she had visited your father and found out that you were still in love with me. That evening I went to the temple to pray to and thank Hanumanji. Bimla came to see me before leaving, and I think she got the hardest slap of her life that day.

"This September I came back home for good as asked by my father. When I arrived with Nancy, my parents were taken aback because they thought we'd got married, but when I cleared the confusion, my father informed me that you were in Dalhousie and would soon join a hospital in Shimla. He told me in private about the house they'd built for us and I decided I would not let Nancy stay there, so we stayed at the hotel Alisia. Then he told me with a wink that he had sold his old cottage in Shimla to 'Khanna Sahib'."

A servant came in to tell them dinner was ready, and they proceeded to the dining room. It was late at night when he told her to go home and get some sleep because they were leaving early the next morning for Shimla.

Just as she was about to leave, the phone rang. Karan picked it up and said, "Hello Pamela! How are you?" He was quiet as the person on the line spoke and then he said, "Yes, Krina is here with me after so long. Yes, we're still in love, and perhaps more so than before!" He spoke to her briefly before hanging up. He turned to Krina and took her hands in his. "It makes me so happy to tell everyone that we're finally together." He kissed her.

"What about my diary?" Krina asked.

"It was with me in Boston, and now it will remain with me forever. It is one thing I must ask you never to touch. One day when I have a son, I will tell him how this small diary became such a large part of our love".

# Chapter 6

Back at her cottage the next morning the phone rang. Krina looked at her clock. Six *o'clock? Why on earth is Karan calling this early?* Thinking something must surely be wrong she sat up alarmed. "What is it? What happened?"

"Wake up, sleepyhead," came his cheerful voice, "be ready by eight. We're not going to Shimla today, we're going somewhere else."

"What? Where?"

"I'll tell you on the way. I need to go to Mumbai, but I'm happy that we still have two more days before I have to leave. Don't worry about any arrangements; I have had Ram Singh inform your nanny and she will leave for Shimla with your driver at ten o'clock." He hung up before she could demand any more information.

With a yawn she lay back in bed thinking of the previous night, and how she felt like she was glowing when Karan had answered the phone and told his American friend about her. She felt so fortunate to have a man like him in love with her. Her father always said that the blue-blooded royals, even if they were now ex-royals, observed traditions,customs and family norms very strictly, and that was his only reason for feeling concerned. He didn't know how she would adjust to their society, but he believed that if their love were true, nothing else mattered. She had faith in Karan, but the deep look in his brown eyes made her doubt whether what she saw was reality or a dream!

She finally climbed out of bed a little while later knowing Karan to be very punctual, and sure enough, at 8 am sharp his white Benz entered the gate and stopped in front of her cottage. Her nanny handed a day bag she had packed for Krina to Karan's driver, Bahadur, who got out of the car to put it in the boot.

Karan looked Krina up and down till she grew conscious and demanded, "What?"

"Nothing, it just seems that you have begun grooming yourself to impress me; you're now wearing modern clothes instead of those tribal ones you're so fond of. But what you don't know is that I loved you even when you were in your simple Pahari langur attire!" He affectionately stroked her left cheek with his lips and then went on to say, "So, last night my father called and told me to take you to the Valley View Hotel and watch the sunrise and sunset with you there."

"Oh, did you also speak to your mother? How is she?"

"Better now, the angioplasty she was scheduled for has been postponed for two days because they want more tests done. But anyway, the reason my father wanted me to take you there is because he thinks we should be together for these two days and I should take you to all the places that I had always wanted to, to share all the beautiful views I thought of you while seeing."

"But where is this Valley View Hotel?"

"Wait and see," he grinned. "I've been thinking about that handsome college friend of yours who is so in love with you that he wouldn't even marry. I am, of course, jealous, but I'm glad I got you in time!" Bahadur climbed into the car and Karan told him, "Kandaghat, and then to Chail." He started the car but Krina's nanny came back running. There was a phone call from Krina's parents in London.

Krina rushed back into the house and picked up the phone. "Hello?"

It was her father. "So Krina has finally been reunited with her Karan, has she?" He chuckled, "I'm so happy for you both. I won't tell your mother anything yet till it is official and you can tell her yourself."

"But who –" Krina started to say, but her father had already hung up. She went back to the car and told Karan about the call.

"It's possible that my father told him," he said and cut her off before she could say anything further, "now enough, just sit back and relax."

The car pulled out of the gate, turned right at Kumar Hati and made its way to the Solan bypass. It was a wide, steep road but it had the most magnificent view of the grassy slope, the deep gorge and the snowy streams that cut across the valleys and forested hills under the backdrop of the high mountains. There were scattered houses with red tiled roofs, and Karan pointed out that there were many fruit orchards and vegetable gardens that grew tomatoes and potatoes besides rice there.

They had almost climbed the top of the mountain when Karan said that they were going to the Chail, the other hill station built by the Maharaja of Patiala before they reached the Valley View Hotel, the resort owned by his father, for lunch. He had invested a lot in the hotel and his main purpose was to attract foreign tourists and give them one of the most breathtaking views of the sunrise and sunset. "Every time I came to Kasauli I wished I could have taken you there," he said.

They left the main highway at Kandaghat about 18 kms from Solan and took a narrow road that twisted and turned its way to Chail, at an altitude of 2226m above sea level. It is a small town built by the Maharaja of Patilala upon being forbidden from entering Shimla by Lord Kitchener, the commander-in-chief of the British army in the 1890s. Rumour has it that they fought because when he was younger, Maharaja Bhupinder Singh had a brief affair with the commander's daughter, for which Lord Kitchener demanded an apology but the Maharaja refused. As Kitchener barred his entry to Shimla, he created another hill station even higher than Shimla and named it Chail. Initially he had chosen a different spot, but it is said that it was the place a saint had meditated long ago and had come to him in a dream to tell him not to build his palace there. Instead, he built the Sidh Baba temple on that spot, and chose a different location for Chail where he built a magnificent palace for his family, which his son later demolished and turned into a fort now known as Raj Garh, or 'the fort of the ruler'. Today that fort has been converted into a resort with massive lawns and orchards called Chail Palace Hotel. The Maharaja was a keen cricketer, leading the first Indian cricket team to England in 1911, and he built the world's highest cricket ground about 2 kms from the present hotel at the altitude of 2444 m, though sometimes the mist was said to become so thick that the players could not even see the ball.

Krina looked at the twisted climb, most of the view obscured by the dense oak and deodar forest no one was allowed to cut down, leading to the town that crowned the top of the mountain nestled in a tranquil sylvan paradise.

They reached the Palace Hotel and decided to have tea in its lush lawns. Bahadur told them that in the town's wildlife sanctuary one could see a variety of animals like the khalij and chir pheasants, and the goral, barking, and sambar deer, and there was also fishing at a spot 29km away along the Gaura river. It certainly sounded inviting but they decided to continue on their way to the Valley View Hotel.

Krina spent some time in the local market buying jewellery and shawls, and the two of them went to see the cricket ground, which had now become a playground for schoolboys. It was past 2 pm when they finally left Chail for Kufri where along the way they could see the beautiful Choor Chandini peak. They drove for at least 15 kms before they saw the board for the Valley View Hotel. The road that took them off the highway was steep and narrow with twists and turns to the right on a rocky slope with few trees. Then suddenly it led to a wide, open expanse that overlooked the valley, the distant Dhaula Dhars and the snow-covered hills of Shimla. Peeping through tall trees that had been planted in avenues was a three-storey white building with a green roof. The car pulled into the driveway and stopped in front of the stairs.

Krina stepped out and breathed in the fresh mountain air and marvelled at the openness of the view the solitary hill provided. In the lawns, tables and garden umbrellas had been put up and guests were enjoying the view. Karan explained that the suite in the right corner of the hotel on the third floor, the Pink Suite, was always reserved for personal use.

"I brought Nancy here on our way to Kasauli and I was in a hurry to get there so I was prepared to leave after tea, but the manager, Raj Kuman, the fool that he was, started talking about the sunrise and the sunset. That's when I learnt that she did have feelings for me because she took my hand and insisted that we stay. Then she had the guts to kiss me on my cheek! I knew I would be a fool to mistake her for a simple woman. When I refused to stay, for the first time in our travel together she began to throw tantrums and refused to talk to me. It taught me never to think of women as the innocent sex," he laughed. A man hurried over to them. "Raj Kumar, this is Krina, my fiancé," Karan introduced.

Raj Kumar touched her feet and said, "*Bade sahib* just informed us that you would be coming. Please, follow me." Krina smiled and she and Karan made their way inside the hotel, where from between the pillars at the entrance one could still see the beauty of the valley. The wide staircase led to a covered verandha with a polished wooden floor. Inside there was a very spacious restaurant full of people, the open bay windows that overlooked the other side of the valley with a view equally breathtaking. The restaurant had a dance floor and a bar where soft music was playing. Krina thought that she couldn't blame Nancy for her actions because the environment was just so romantic.

"Let's go to our suite," Karan said. Krina followed him to the third floor. The view from the window was that of the terrace gardens and the lawns that had fountains and beautiful, neat flowerbeds, where guests lounged under the garden umbrellas. In the distance they saw the Shimla hills and Karan told her that's where they would see the sunrise before they left the next day. "Tomorrow when I wake you up for the sunrise, you will see the entire valley shrouded in mist," he murmured. Then remembering he had only one more day before he had to go to Mumbai, he said,

"I hate the thought of being separated from you."

After lunch they sat in front of the grate where a fire was burning and he told her about his life in America. "When I look back today, I think our parents were wise in separating us. I got admission to the same college as you in Delhi; my father forced me to study abroad. The reason he gave at the time was that he wanted me to be away from the tag of royalty and my vast inheritance and become someone in my own right. So he let me pursue medicine, but in America. It was my first visit abroad. Everything in Boston had been arranged by a close friend of his, Mr Ram Chaudha, who had been with him at Bishop Cotton School, Shimla and Mayo College, Lahore. When he left India to go to America he became a well-known architect and married a woman there named Margaret Rice. They were a childless couple but very affectionate. He was my local guardian, and arranged a two-bedroom apartment in the posh area of town for me, where an Anglo-Indian couple, David and Helen John attended to me. I also had a Mercedes Benz with a chauffeur but I was not allowed to drive because my father was overprotective. I was comfortable, but so much happier when Ram Singh came to Boston to look after me. From then on, I made up my mind to stand on my own feet as a professional, rather than be known by my ex-royal title.

"The only thing I had to remember you by was a photograph that was by my bed and when I went out of the house, in my wallet. It's a snap by Devi Chand of you when you fell and gestured at me like a langur."

"Karan..." She pulled him closer and kissed him.

He chuckled and said, "Royal would-be brides never display their feelings openly like this, but my Krina is different. You know, American girls are not only very bold but sometimes difficult to resist," he pinched her nose, "but I was always true to my love, and never lost sight of my goal, which was to be with you and to stand on my own feet. Life in medical school in America was tough; the only leave I got was in October when I came to India for a fortnight to attend the Founder's Day. Bimla would always come and speak to me though she was wasting her time, and I relied only on Kanta to hear news of you. So till I finally met you, I kept up my interest in riding, and for the first time even took up golfing. I worked hard to be successful and the first girl I met once I started working was Kamla Sharma, a nurse. She was very simple and hard working, always ready to work late. She used to stare at me sometimes and I wondered what was going on but when I visited her house, I found out that it was because I looked a lot like her brother who had been a pilot in the Indian Air Force and had died during the Indo-Pak conflict in Kashmir. I even met her parents who were doctors before they retired and really liked them. Kamla got married to a lawyer in Singapore and left America. Later during my residency, I met a New Zealander, George Smith who had come to America to be a plastic surgeon. The two of us became very good friends and I even told him about you. We took up skiing, and occasionally went for ski vacations to the Alps.

"By that time, though, I was getting very disheartened, thinking that I would probably never meet you again, till I met Kanta who told me that you were coming back to Shimla to work in a hospital there. I was overjoyed when I heard that and told my father about it. Meanwhile, he was getting sick of my mother's nagging to get me to settle down, so that was the end of Boston, my parents asked me to come back home. Today I finally understand why my father sent me away. He wanted me to work hard and become someone before thinking of love and marriage."

Krina once again fell asleep on his arm as did he soon after, and she woke up a few hours later when he stroked her hair. "Oh, what happened?" she felt confused.

"I think it was the heavy meal we had. We both fell asleep in front of the fire. My arm is completely numb, I think that's what woke me up."

"Oh, sorry!" Krina suddenly sat up.

Karan rubbed his arm trying to get some feeling back into it as he walked over to the window. "Now come see, the sun is about to set."

They stood side by side waiting for the sun to set when Krina said, "Karan, close your eyes."

"Why?"

"Just do it!" He did, and she took off the golden chain she wore and put it around his neck. "Now open your eyes." It was a gold chain with a gold pendant on which her name was engraved. "My father gave it to me when I went abroad."

Karan kissed the pendant and said, "I'm going to wear it right here, over my heart."

"Just as the ring on my finger will always remind me that you are there for me, you must promise me you'll never take this chain off unless you stop loving me." Both smiled and Krina looked out the window. The sky was a sober orange, which was slowly giving way to a deep mauve as the sun set. "Karan," she whispered, "every time I see a sunset, I will think of you."

They had dinner in the restaurant and enjoyed the dance and folk song that was the night's entertainment before retiring to bed.

A phone call in the middle of the night woke her up. It was 2 am. She wondered who would call at that hour. She heard Karan answer it in the sitting room outside her bedroom, and feared it might be serious, so she climbed out of bed to see what the matter was.

He sat in front of the fire, his head in his hands. He looked up when Krina came out of her room. "I'm really sorry if the phone woke you up."

"What's wrong? Who was that?"

"Father." He took her hand as she sat down next to him. "It looks as though being with you is not as easy as I thought."

"But what happened?" she asked. "Is your mother all right?"

"Yes, she's fine, there's just some trouble with the Thali family. I spent so long waiting for you, and now that I have you, I can't bear to be parted from you even for a day! I have to go to Mumbai. Father said that we have to postpone our wedding for a few weeks." Then he said suddenly, "Why not get married now, before I leave for Mumbai?"

"Do you really want that?"

"Yes, I do."

"All right, let's do it," Krina said putting her head on his shoulder.

He smiled when he looked down at her, because she had fallen asleep.

The next morning she got dressed early so she and Karan could watch the sunrise together. "Look," Karan said, and Krina turned to him. "With this rising sun we're getting married, albeit somewhat unconventionally." He cut his thumb slightly with a knife and marked the parting in her hair with it. "When in the morning you look at the sun in my absence, remember that we are separated only briefly, and that we are now bound by this blood." He kissed her and then they held each other as they watched the sun rise from behind the Choor Chandini. Finally there was a knock on his door that meant he had to leave, as it was time for his flight. "Remember that Karan belongs only to Krina," he said. "This ring and this blood is proof of that promise."

At the Jabarhatti airport he hugged her and said, "Remember I have promised never to take off this chain as you have promised, the ring. These are the symbols of our trust and faith in each other." Though he smiled, Krina knew something was wrong. She watched him leave and then went back into the car, where she found an envelope marked 'Thali'. She pulled out the letter left for her by Karan. It read:

*Krina, whenever you feel sad, think of me and know that I will be thinking of you. Remember this verse from* The Way of White Clouds *by Lama Anaganika Govinda called 'Song of the Eastern Snow Mountain':*

On the peak of the white snow mountains of the East.
A white cloud seams to be rising towards the sky
At the instances of beholding it, I remember my teacher
And, pondering over his kindness, faith stirs in me"

*So, Krina, there is some mild turbulence in our happy union but I am confident we will make it through, if you have faith in me. – Karan.*

She re-read the letter and decided that come what may, she would never for a moment lose faith in him. When she reached her cottage, Bahadur told her, “Sahib has told me to always be at your service, madam. I have left my address with your nanny. If you ever need anything of me, just send word.”

# Chapter 7

Krina left her cottage in Chhota Shimla at 9 am on her first day at the new private hospital, Padmawati Institute of Medical Sciences and Research, close to Mashobra. When she started to explain the directions to her driver, he said, "Madam, I know where the hospital is, I took my mother there once for an operation."

"Really?" Krina was quite surprised. "It must have been very expensive!"

"No, madam, some of the cases are treated free of cost for the poor. The hospital is run by a rich royal family in some state near Rampur."

The day was clear but cold though the trees were as beautiful as ever, and the fragrance of pine still lingered in the air. The car turned on the national highway toward Tatapani and passed by the brightest wildflowers Krina had seen and she shut her eyes to listen to the music of the mountains. Everything was beautiful, but knew it would be even more so if she had Karan to share it with.

She leaned back and let her head fall against the headrest. It had been over a week since Karan had left for Mumbai but he hadn't contacted her yet. She wondered what was so wrong that he hadn't found the time to even call. She admired his control over his emotions, true to his suraj-wanshi descent. She thought back to the few days they had spent together and wondered whether it had all been just a dream.

The car climbed the narrow road uphill between the trees that stood tall on either side and formed an arch blocking most of the sunlight. They reached the gate of the hospital, which the guards opened after enquiring who she was. Their khakhi uniform and the peculiar silk green turbans were almost identical to those of the guards at the house of two Ks that Karan had taken her to. *The hospital probably uses the same security company*, she thought.

She stepped out of the car at the porch and took in the view. There were messy but endearing lawns speckled with differently coloured flowers, and the hospital was at an excellent location with an unencumbered view of the surrounding hills and valley. She knew she was going to love working there.

The hospital was a six-storey building with a green tiled roof. The name 'Padmawati Institute of Medical Science and Research' stood bold above the entrance. At the main door of the hospital she saw more guards wearing the same uniform, and then remembered what her driver had said to her about the hospital being run by someone from Karan's state. *I wonder…no, Karan would have mentioned it. It can't be.* She entered the hospital and stepped into a wide hall with a light grey tiled floor and a ceiling of carved dark teak with chandeliers suspended from it. There was a long wooden desk along one side where three women sat attending to patients. They wore identity cards over their crisp green *saris* with red borders, had similar haircuts and wore makeup and high heels. On the opposite side were comfortable cushioned chairs for waiting patients. There weren't too many people, unlike the Snowdown hospital. She silently remarked at the aesthetics of the hall, which in her opinion looked like the lobby of a five-star hotel. Her father used to say that was important for hospitals to have a very human approach so the patient could forget his or her misery even if only for those few moments while speaking to an attendant. Service was as important in hospitals as in any hotel.

He had been unhappy when Krina had applied to the Snowdown hospital in Shimla and objected by saying, "You've only worked in public hospitals so far. When you come to Shimla, why don't you try working at a private one? Your mother and I will be in Chandigarh, not too far from you. And who knows, one day you just might have a private hospital of your own." Krina had never heard of the Padmawati Institute, but thought that it must be good because it was said to compete with Snowdown.

Krina approached the desk and asked to see Dr Mathur, the head of the Anaesthesia department. The young woman asked for some identity and then made a quick phone call after which she rang a bell. A man in the blue hospital uniform came hurrying over. "Dr Krina Khanna, Vikram will take you to the theatre complex on the fourth floor. Dr Mathur will see you in his office," the woman smiled.

The man led her to the lift, and Krina noticed the stark difference between this hospital and the ones she was used to, which were crowded and often smelled unpleasant. The hospital staff was always overworked and she believed that the general cleanliness was difficult to maintain, what with the patients littering everywhere.

The doors of the lift opened at the 4th floor, which was another wide corridor with bay windows that afforded the same view of the hills that she saw at the entrance of the hospital. She was conducted to a small antechamber where a man, presumably Dr Mathur's secretary, sat. "Come in, doctor sahib is waiting for you," he greeted Krina and ushered her inside the office.

Dr Mathur was sitting behind his desk in the unisex green theatre pajama-kurta. As she walked in, he looked up, set his pen down, rose from his desk and offered her his hand. "Welcome to the hospital. I'm glad you're joining us." He gestured to her with a smile to take a seat. "I'm sure you'll like working here." He called out to Ram Dev to bring in two coffees. "So, tell me, how do you like the hospital so far?"

"The location is very scenic. I love the hills and I couldn't wish for a better workplace. I'm very glad I'm joining you." The coffee arrived in expensive china mugs.

Dr Mathur explained, "The hospital is run by the administrator Mr Bhardwaj but guarded by a senior trustee. In November it will be taken over by his son who is a surgeon and organ transplant specialist from America. You will find that everything in this hospital is very modern and it has the top-of-the-line equipment. There is also enough money in the trust to keep it running smoothly and take good care of our staff. It is only six months old but we've earned a good reputation for ourselves, and the occupancy of beds has now gone up to 5690." They finished their coffee as he told her more about the hospital till a clerk came in to say he was needed for something. Dr Mathur excused himself and left Krina alone in the office.

As she drained the last of her own coffee, she looked around the office. The floor was carpeted and all the furniture was made of teak wood. He had an oval desk with comfortable chairs in front of another bay window where the thick velvet curtains had been drawn apart, and there was a very large painting of a mountain that hung over the fireplace. Krina liked the lavishness of the hospital and appreciated how much had been invested in ensuring the comfort of the doctors.

Dr Mathur came back apologising and continued telling her about the hospital. "The department of surgery and anaesthesia are on the 4th and 5th floors. There are five senior surgeons specialising in plastic, orthopaedics, organ transplant and urology and neurosurgery. In anaesthesia we have three senior consultants: Dr. Bhatia, Dr. Sunil and you. Of course, I am the head of the department, but only till the 15th, when Dr Kumar will take over as chief of surgery, and will also be in charge of the administration. Besides that we have two house surgeons and two junior anaesthesia registrars." He smiled and motioned for Krina to get up and said, "Now let me show you around the theatre complex and introduce you to the sister-in-charge, Shanta Negi, and her three staff nurses, Ms Mehra, Neelam, and Neena who is on leave."

The corridor outside his office had bay windows too, as a constant reminder that one was surrounded by beauty. Dr Mathur noticed Krina looking out of the windows as they passed by and said, "You seem to be a great lover of nature."

"It is truly beautiful," Krina smiled.

They reached a set of glass doors by the theatre. Dr Mathur instructed the nurse to show Krina the changing room and then take her to sister Negi's office. The changing room was quite spacious with personal lockers and green surgical gowns of all sizes and surgical shoes. There were small cabins, in one of which Krina changed.

When she came out she asked the nurse about the sitting room. "Oh, ma'am, there's the surgeons' lounge," she explained and led her in. There was nobody inside. The room's décor was much like Dr Mathur's office. There was yet another bay window in the lounge through which she could see the hospital lawns and the valley and hills beyond them. The nurse pointed and said, "Our trustee's house is there, behind that forest." Krina acquainted herself with the lounge, checking its coffee maker, looking at the expensive crockery and the cookie box. Together she and the nurse went to sister Negi's office just as Dr Mathur was leaving. "I'm sorry, I have a meeting that I must rush to, but sister Negi will look after you today."

Sister Negi welcomed her warmly and asked her to sit down. "Four of the five theatres are closed for cleaning but the one used by Dr Varma, our plastic surgeon, is free and I think you can see the set-up."

Krina accepted and watched the nurse get up. She assumed her to be in her mid-thirties on the plumper side and about 5'4" in height. Her face was broad and long with blunt features and a wheatish complexion, but she had a kind smile. She wore a unisex theatre gown similar to Krina's.

"Come, let's not waste any more time," sister Negi smiled and held the door open for her. She took her to see the theatre, which had the same view of the hills, and then to the recovery room and the small intensive care unit. She told her that there was no use going to have a look at the 5th floor because it was still unfinished; they were making it suitable for the future owner of the hospital.

They were getting the department of organ transplantation ready for him, as he would arrive on 15th November. The sixth floor was for the neurosurgery and cardiology departments. "But if you'd like to see the rest of the hospital as well, it's best we stop for a quick cup of coffee at the surgeons' lounge first." On their way to the lounge, the nurse continued, "This hospital's standards can match those of any hospital, even in England. This is a private hospital so the trustee has spent a lot of money to ensure that it is the best. Dr Mathur is confident that we will become even busier once the chief joins and the urologist is ready. However, so far we don't have a department of gynaecology or paediatrics."

They reached the lounge where this time Krina found two junior nurses and one doctor. Sister Negi introduced them and after having coffee, they set off on a tour of the rest of the hospital. Finally, sister Negi left Krina in what would be her office. Her office was much smaller than Dr Mathur's, but looked almost the same. She relished the view of the snow-capped mountains from her own bay window.

Krina decided to leave early and begin her duties from the following day. Once back at the cottage, she took the nanny's shopping list and went to the Sahib Singh store at the Mall. While she was looking over the list, someone called out from behind her, "Madam!"

She turned around to see Bahadur, Karan's driver. "Bahadur! How are you?"

"I'm well, madam."

"How is everything at Thali?"

"Under control. The royal family is still at Mumbai but *buaji* and Shallu *memsahib* came back here yesterday."

"Oh. Who is Shallu?"

"She is related to them, a doctor working in the Snowdown Hospital. But how are you, madam?"

"I'm fine," Krina smiled.

"I have kept in touch with your nanny to find out if you are comfortable, as instructed by sahib. Now we are waiting for the royal family to return to Shimla but buaji is leaving tomorrow for Thali."

Her heart sank slightly at being reminded of Karan. It had been a week since they parted and Krina wondered what family problem could be so severe that he hadn't found the time to call her even once. There was something about Shallu's being in Mumbai with his buaji that made her somewhat suspicious though she couldn't quite put a finger on it. *Maybe Shallu is the cause of the family problem?*

She ran her finger over the parting in her hair remembering the blood he had used for *sindoor* and the ring he had slipped onto her finger promising that nothing would ever separate them. On her way home, however, the more she thought of this Shallu, the more she managed to convince herself that she was clearly the reason Karan hadn't called yet, although it didn't make any sense because Karan had never mentioned her before.

It was a couple of weeks later that she recovered from a bout of viral pneumonia under the care of Dr Pradeep Sharma. On the day Dr Sharma discharged her he examined her X-ray carefuly and chided her saying, "You can go home now, but really, doctors and nurses not knowing better than to go out in a snowstorm! You were a hair's breadth away from entering the domain of Lord Yama. I want to you stay home, rest and remember: absolutely *no* exertion or exposure to the cold. Don't let me hear that you've been taking walks or gone horse riding."

It was an ironic start to her career at the hospital, being admitted in it herself for a week and a half, having caught pneumonia when she'd gone out in a snowstorm to help sisters Karuna and Neelam whose car had struck a tree on the narrow road along the slope to Kufri.

It had also been more than a couple of weeks since she'd heard from Karan. When her friend Sunita, a skin specialist at Snowdown had come to see her at the hospital, Krina had asked about Shallu.

She quickly made up the excuse of wanting to know a good cardiologist in Shimla since she knew she would be living there for a while.

"She must be in her thirties but I've heard she had plastic surgery done in London, so she looks twenty. Everyone at Snowdown considers her a snob. She's the widow of some royal at Rampur," Sunita said, "though if you want a competent cardiologist, I'd suggest Dr Tripathi."

Krina nodded and didn't disclose the real reason she had asked. As per the doctor's instructions, Krina did not indulge in any heavy physical activity, but did take up some light duties at the hospital. She had grown fond of the staff and enjoyed her work even though Karan's silence still troubled her. She had slowly resigned herself to the idea that the few days they spent together had been too good to be true and her real future did not have Karan in it.

She had been feeling doubly alone since he'd left for Mumbai because even her parents' stay in the UK had been prolonged when her uncle's operation had been postponed. Sensing her anxiety, her colleagues tried their best to keep her spirits up. Dr Varma, especially, would ensure that he did whatever he could to make her laugh and lighten up her mood. But as the weather worsened, she fell sick again. This time she decided not to go to Dr Sharma but treat herself with anitbiotics.

It was late in the evening when staff Karuna rang Krina that she had met the new chief of Surgery. He came to look at his office at on fifth floor. She was leaving but sister Negi told me to wait.

Soon, a blue Mercedes-Benz pulled up and a tall handsome young man in his late twenties stepped out. He was casually dressed in an English grey tweed coat, matching corduroy trousers and a green polo-neck woollen skivvy.

He was introduced by Dr. Bhardwaj. Yes, Krina he was too handsome but very pleasant man! It was sister who told me to get keys of his office from theatre. When I returned I saw Mr. Kumar was deep in conversation with Mr Bhardwaj, the administrator, and they waited while sister Negi unlocked his office. and I left.

On my way back down, a woman stopped her and asked if she could help her find Dr Kumar's office. "I'm Dr Shallu," she introduced herself.

I pointed towards the elevator and dreading the reply, asked, "Mrs Kumar?"

She smiled mysteriously and said before walking away, "Not just yet."

On 15th November morning they met Dr Kumar in the reception and Dr Shallu was there.

Dr Varma caught Krina returning to her office and asked, "Krina, how are you feeling? You're looking quite pale." He looked at Shallu entering the lift. "I see you've met Dr Shallu. How do you find her?"

"Haughty," Krina said without discretion, "I heard she had plastic surgery done to remove her wrinkles. Did you notice how she covers her flaws with makeup?"

"Like a plastic doll, then?" Dr Varma laughed as he strolled to his own office.

"I wonder how soon she'll be occupying the office next to Dr Kumar's," Krina narrowed her eyes at the lift. She wanted to be the one working with Karan. If her heart raced at just his touch, she wondered what effect he would have on the rest of the female staff.

Feeling anxiety swell up inside her she realised she had been unconsciously playing with the ring he gave her. For a brief moment she blamed her father for suggesting the job to her but immediately felt guilty for the thought. He couldn't possibly have known that the hospital belonged to Karan's family. Then she wondered whether the blame should be directed at Karan. He had known she was joining a hospital in Shimla, so he must have known which one! Why hadn't he said anything? She had to settle the matter once and for all. The least he owed her was an explanation.

Before confronting him she gave him a chance to find her and explain himself, but he didn't. Late one afternoon when she was in the surgeons' lounge, she heard his voice and immediately turned her head to see. Her heart melted when she saw how handsome and charming he looked, and it missed a beat when he looked in her direction and smiled. She opened her mouth to say something when the woman he was actually smiling at, a nurse standing next to Krina stepped forward. He completely ignored Krina and asked the nurse to find sister Negi for him, and left.

Krina's mouth was still half open when another nurse said, "Krina? What's the matter?"

She checked herself and said, "Nothing."

"That was Dr Kumar, our chief of surgery. You know, he thought you were a nurse, but I told him you were a senior anaesthetist!" She smiled. "I'm making coffee for myself. Do you want me to make some for you as well?"

"No, thanks, I. . .have to attend to a patient," Krina made a hurried exit and went to her office. Feeling insulted she picked up the phone and dialled the direct line in Karan's office. He answered but when Krina said, "Karan," she heard the sound of the phone being moved around, some muffled voices, and then his secretary was on the line. "Hello, Dr Khanna? I'm so sorry but Dr Kumar has said that he is not to be disturbed on his direct line. If you're facing any sort of problem, the person you need to speak to is Dr Mathur. If you still wish to speak to Dr Kumar then you'll have to make an appointment with me."

Resenting this slap in the face, she charged into his office though his secretary tried to bar the way. She opened the door to a very surprised-looking Shallu who was seated on the sofa before the fireplace holding a cup of tea, and the smile that had been on Karan's lips died. "What is the meaning of this?" he demanded. "How dare you!" He didn't let Krina respond. "Ram Prasad! What is she doing here?" Krina stood speechless as Ram Prasad came and shut the door. "Madam, please," he said helplessly. The last thing she saw was Karan bending down to say something to Shallu who laughed.

On the verge of tears, she locked herself in her office and made some excuse to Karan's secretary about looking for some keys and not knowing he was in the office in a weak effort to prevent the entire hospital from gossiping about her. She did not emerge from her office till she was sure she had regained her composure. When she returned to her office at the end of the day to collect her things, Ram Prasad was inside, placing an envelope on her desk. "Madam, sir has sent this for you."

She smiled tightly and thanked him, opening the letter as soon as he left.

Written in Karan's bold handwriting, the letter read:

*Dr Khanna,*

*I am writing this letter to let you know that circumstances are no longer as you knew them to be. You may not be aware of our customs and traditions, so allow me to inform you that royal blood only marries royal blood to ensure the purity in our line, and Dr Shallu is of a good lineage. I apologise for not having intimated this to you earlier, but Dr Shallu and I are to be married soon. I will greatly appreciate it if you understand.*

*I must stress the need for you to treat our relationship as a purely professional one if you wish to continue working here. I would also like you to address me as 'Dr Kumar' in future. I must warn you that I will not entertain any more attempts to invade my privacy or any other sort of retaliation; you will only end up harming yourself. I promise you that I will take particular care to keep our interaction at a complete minimum.*

*I assure you that your personal future is no concern of mine.*

*I leave the rest to your discretion.*

*Dr Kumar*

With fresh tears clouding her vision, Krina remembered how her father had once warned her about blue blood marrying only its own kind. How could she have been so foolish to think she and Karan had a future together?

Defeated, she sat down at her desk and let her tears flow, only being brought back to reality with the ringing of her phone. "Hello?"

"Krina! It's Rajinder!"

"Rajinder?" she blinked.

"What are you still doing at work? It's late!" he said cheerfully. "So anyway, I'm in Shimla only for tonight, and I want to see you. Come to the Clark Hotel at 8 o'clock."

"But…"

"No, I don't want to hear anything; I'm off to Kashmir for two weeks tomorrow and I want to see you."

Krina wiped her tears and agreed, put her things together and left.

The only thing she could think of on her drive back was the humiliation she suffered. Receiving that letter had been even worse than being thrown out of his office. '*I assure you that your personal future is no concern of mine.*' She gave out an involuntary sob. He had even threatened to fire her if she didn't behave professionally. She shook her head as she neared her house. *Perhaps dinner with Rajinder would take my mind off things. He always makes me laugh.*

At home, she took the advice of her Australian friend, Margaret, who had said, "When I'm feeling really low, I pamper myself with a hot bubble bath, put on my best dress, do up my hair and go out for the night."

So Krina pushed her worries aside and got ready to meet Rajinder. She pulled out her new black pashmina Kulu dress embroidered with red and green motifs, a matching scarf and ruby earrings.

After getting dressed she admired herself in the mirror and was pleased with her appearance. The dress showed off her slim and tall figure, and complemented her black eyes and shoulder-length hair. Her eyes were no longer red and puffy from crying and Margaret's advice came back to her: *life is for living, not for weeping. Fight with so much courage that your adversaries can only worry about your next move.*

She was already 15 minutes late for dinner so she hurried to the hotel. She felt calm but wondered whether she'd be able to maintain her composure if she saw Karan and Shallu together again. She was torn between loving Karan and hating his betrayal. Feeling the worry beginning to creep back into her mind, she forcefully pushed it aside again and put on a bright smile to greet Rajinder.

# Chapter 8

At 8.30 the lobby of the hotel bustled with tourists and Krina couldn't see Rajinder anywhere. She waited for a few minutes and then went to the restroom to check her appearance once again. She was happy to note that her eyes did not at all seem as if she had been crying though her cheeks did appear a little pale, so she applied some rouge. Involuntarily she touched the parting in her hair that Karan had marked with his blood and decided it was time to let herself heal, but inside she knew that she could never heal from the wound he'd given her. Tears sprang to her eyes and she prayed to Hanuman to give her the strength to make it through.

After she had satisfactorily dried her tears and regained her cool, she left the restroom and found a hotel employee searching for her. "Madam, are you Dr Krina?" he asked. When she nodded he said, "Mr Rajinder Singh is waiting for you in the restaurant."

She followed him to the restaurant where Rajinder greeted her at the entrance. "Krina," he said softly.

She turned around to see her old friend in his wing commander's uniform looking as tall and dashing as ever. "My, aren't we looking handsome today," she smiled.

He looked her up and down. "You look so beautiful yourself that no words can do you justice," he bowed to her in the Lucknowi fashion and then with an arm around her waist, guided her to their table. He first helped her into her chair and then sat down, taking her hand. "Krina, you make my heart race." She blushed and turned her head to face the window in an effort to avoid looking at him. Quickly, to change the subject, she said, "Look how beautiful Shimla is at night."

He refused to look away from her and smiled. "What do I need to look at Shimla for when you're sitting in front of me?" Krina blushed even more deeply. He too was of a royal lineage and was just as flirtatious as Karan, and just as popular with women, but that's where the similarities ended. "You're too flippant!" she told him.

The soft music in the background made the ambience very pleasant, and even though it was quite full only a murmur of voices was audible. Krina looked around at the other tables when her heart skipped a beat. At one of the tables sat Karan with Shallu. Shallu was dressed provocatively in a thin black chiffon sari that amply displayed her beautiful marble-like body beneath. They were sitting with a man who Krina could not identify. Trying to hide her face yet again, she turned to Rajinder who asked, "Is something wrong?"

"Oh, no, not at all."

"You're very quiet all of a sudden. Are you all right? I heard about your pneumonia. How are you feeling now?"

"Much better, though I haven't completely recovered. I still have a cough. Mustn't laugh too much," she smiled. Determined not to look at Karan, she resolved to devote her full attention to Rajinder but found herself thinking of the insult Karan had delivered for the woman who sat opposite him.

"Still a dreamer, aren't you?" Rajinder laughed. "You're forever lost in your own thoughts."

She laughed. "I'm sorry." When the waiter came to take their order, she asked for some warm water with lemon, sugar, and a pinch of salt. "I have to avoid cold drinks."

"I can see you've made an effort to look good tonight, but I can also see you're still ill." He looked at her in earnest and clasped her hand. "Krina, why don't you let me look after you? You know I love you. Why don't you give me a chance? I must have asked you a hundred times by now."

"You've asked only ten times," Krina laughed, extricating her hand from his grasp. "I'm sorry, but my answer is still 'no'." The wound

Karan had delivered was still so raw. *How can anyone who loves someone insult her so much?*

"Why? Can't we try to be together for six months before you give me your answer? I promise I can look after you."

"Rajinder..."

The drinks arrived and Rajinder changed the subject, engaging her in stories about Leh and how it was difficult to survive there without drinks.

"Kumar Rajinder Singh?" someone clapped his shoulder. The man who had been sitting with Karan and Shallu was now at their table.

Rajinder rose up and warmly shook hands with him. "Of course, Rana Negi sahib!" he turned to Krina and said, "Sahib, this is Dr Krina. Krina, this is Major Negi. He was with me at Leh." Krina greeted him politely. He was tall and muscular, but she could see he was also developing a paunch. "Please, sahib, join us," Rajinder said.

"I'd love to, but I'm here with my sister and her fiancé." He turned to Krina. "Ma'am, when we saw you, my sister Dr Shallu told me that you're an upcoming folk singer, and how you two met at Kala near Dalhousie."

"How we met?" Krina was confused. She had never seen Shallu before the day she met her in the hospital.

"Yes, there was a snowstorm outside, but you kept everyone stuck inside the hotel entertained with your melodious voice," he smiled. "You made quite a few fans that day. Please, come and meet my sister. She is a heart specialist at Snowdown. And that's her fiancé, Dr Kumar. Dr Kumar has joined his own hospital as a surgeon. He will be the first organ transplant specialist in this state!"

Rajinder and he made small talk for a minute or two more and then he wished them both a pleasant evening and left for his own table.

"What a bore," Krina said when she saw the major sit down and Karan glance over at her.

"Both brother and sister are the children of the former ruler of Pratap Garh of Lower Kinnaur, but they are now penniless and just survive on their reputation. They may be ex-royals, but I've heard they've blackmailed people a few times. His sister is too old for her fiancé; she's had plastic surgery done to look the way she looks."

"I wonder if he knows that," Krina muttered as Karan looked discreetly in her direction once more.

"I don't know if it matters to him," Rajinder winked, "he seems to be a flirt with a roving eye."

"It takes one to know one!" Krina teased. They both laughed, and she stole a glance at Karan. He was now looking fixedly at them.

The food was served, and in the middle of their meal, an old couple came up to them. The man introduced himself as Colonel Mehra and said that his wife had pointed out to him that Krina was a wonderful singer and that they would love to have her sing a few lines of 'Dhuru' for them.

Krina apologised, telling them about her illness and that her doctor had asked her not to sing.

"Oh, I'm very sorry to hear that. I don't mean to force you, but it's just that it's our 25th anniversary today," he smiled apologetically.

"Oh, well, in that case, let me sing a few lines to offer you my congratulations."

She ascended the stage and whispered to the musicians who nodded and prepared to play the music she needed. She took the microphone and said, "I'd like to wish Colonel and Mrs Mehra a very happy anniversary and all the best for the future." She cleared her throat and began the first verse of the song of the dance of Lord Shiva.

Dhuru Nachia Jatta bho khillari oh.
Nache Dhurua abh teri bari ho.
Dhuru Nachia, oh Dhuru Nachia.

There was a cough and she stopped and then started again.

Ganga Gora nahne jo chali ho.
Boli Gora to kia meri lagdi ho.
Ganga boli sonkan teri ho.
Ganga Goa sara sara pete ho
Ganga Gora Sara Sara pete ho
Dhuru Nachia jatta bo khillari ho

Nachay Dhurua –

She couldn't complete the line because she was overcome by a fit of coughing. Everyone in the restaurant applauded anyway, and she got off stage smiling. The couple came up to her. Mrs Mehra pressed a glass of warm water in her hands and both thanked her heartily.

Rajinder stood up for her when she returned to the table and said, "I wish you had asked me to come up and sing with you."

"Oh, I completely forgot!" Krina said. Rajinder was also a very good singer.

"Maybe we can sing something else together," he said, gesturing at the stage.

Krina smiled but politely refused, telling him that she had strained her throat enough for the evening.

He leaned forward as she finished the last of the warm water. "You know, Krina," he said, "I think you'd rethink your answer to me if I were to spend more time with you, to stay close to you for a while."

Krina laughed good-naturedly and repeated, "No."

"Well, keep my offer in mind," he said and resumed eating.

Their coffee had just arrived when Karan, Shallu and the major got up to leave. Rajinder commented as Karan helped Shallu put on her coat, "It seems as though this time she's found a good catch. He's handsome and young, and seems very rich." The three walked over to Krina's and Rajinder's table. The major said, "Ma'am, I'm sorry but my sister dearly wanted to meet you."

"Of course," Krina set her cup down and got up to shake hands with Shallu.

"I saw you in the hospital but I didn't recognise you then, and not even when you came into Karan's office."

"I do apologise for invading your privacy," Krina said. "I had no idea he was in that day," Krina said, hastily giving her the story she had made up about looking for some keys because a patient was critical and his reports needed to be accessed.

"Oh no, not at all! In fact, I am sorry. Karan was so rude to you that day!" Shallu exclaimed. "Please, let me formally introduce you.

This is Dr Karan, my fiancé."

Karan stretched his hand out to shake Krina's, but she coldly ignored it, sitting back down to raise her cup to her lips. An awkward silence followed and Rajinder quickly took Karan's hand and introduced himself. The three took their leave and left Rajinder to look at Krina, puzzled. "You were very rude," he said.

"Was I?" Krina said bitterly.

"But he was quite a strange fellow himself. I don't know if the brother and sister duo will be successful in whatever plans they have for him" Rajinder went on, apparently oblivious to Krina's tone. "He had the guiltiest look on his face, though, when you were apologising to him. Are you sure you don't know him?"

"We work at the same hospital."

"Yes, but other than that. There was something about the way he looked at you," he persisted.

Wanting to avoid the topic, Krina laughed and distracted him with a story about the hospital.

That night she returned home late, and to her surprise, woke up in the morning clutching Karan's photograph.

She reached the hospital a little after eight, feeling more confident. She had managed to keep her composure and had even snubbed Karan the night before, and she felt more optimistic about her future. Waking up holding his picture had punctured her happiness a little, but she had decided that it was a habit that she would be rid of only slowly.

Sister Negi told her that Karan had changed the timings of the hospital staff to 9.30 and for the surgery staff to 10 am. This was appreciated because it was difficult to drive in the early morning fog. As she reflected on this, she was convinced that leaving everything aside, she was glad that they had an administrator who had come from a newer school of thought. She anticipated more changes for the better in the future.

She opened her locker and emptied the contents of her bag in it and noticed that the letter was still there. She paused and momentarily contemplated tearing it up, but then she decided not to, wanting to keep it as a reminder of how hurtful love could be, how she had waited eight years for a man who had cheated and insulted her.

With a heavy heart she pulled on her cap and mask and passed by Dr Mathur and Karan who were discussing something outside the men's changing room. She tried to avoid them, but Dr Mathur called out to her. "I've been told that you haven't gone for a follow-up since you were discharged," he frowned.

"I'm sorry, I will definitely go to Dr Sharma," before he had a chance to say anything else, she excused herself and escaped. She spent a busy morning attending to a case, and when she left to go to the lounge for a break, Dr Varma fell in step with her. "So what do you think of our new chief of surgery?" he asked.

"What good is it to think about him? I think we should leave him to his work, and do ours."

"I'm wondering what word I can use to describe you to him which will show him how nice you have been to me," Dr Varma said. "I'm trying to translate Bihiari into English."

Krina laughed. "You let me know how that comes along."

"This is the first time I've seen you laugh all morning."

"That's because you're very good to me."

"We were all very worried when you were ill and prayed for you."

"I'm grateful for that. I felt so alone."

"Don't ever feel alone, Krina," he said affectionately. "Even if there is no one with you, remember that God is."

Feeling a sob rise in her throat, she said, "I'm just going to change. Please, start without me and I'll be right with you." She ducked into the women's changing room and cried softly once inside.

When she finally entered the lounge, she saw Dr Varma ready with a cup of coffee for her as well. Over the weeks she had noticed how fond the staff was of Dr Varma and his comic antics. He gestured towards her and said, "Coffee with sugar! And, I found a word for you, and then I thought of another one to add to it."

"No, I think one word would suffice."

"All right, then. Here it is: adorable," he laughed when she smiled. "I knew you'd admire my flowery English." He passed her a cup.

"Don't tell my wife, but I love working with you." He sipped his own coffee. "You see, when I was courting her she was sweet like honey. Then when we got engaged, the honey was mixed with pepper. Now that we are married, it is all pepper, no honey." Everyone laughed. Krina looked around and stiffened when she noticed Karan bending over the register. Dr Varma peered at Krina's cup. "That's a lot of sugar in such a small cup," but he shook his head and repeated with a smile, "adorable."

She received a call from casualty and made for the lift where Dr Mathur and Karan, clad in their scrubs, joined her. "Krina," Dr Mathur said as they waited for the lift. "What is the need for you to overwork yourself? This isn't an emergency case; it is only a cut tendon. Sunil can easily handle it."

"I'm fine, sir," she insisted. Dr Mathur left her to her work but Karan entered the lift with her. They were alone. "Press ground floor for me," he said. She did it, but made no comment. "I found out you were very sick. How are you now?" Krina still didn't reply. "Won't you tell me?" She was still silent. She felt his temper rise. "Krina, you're making me angry! God, you're so stubborn! Talk, damn you!"

Krina still held her tongue, and was rescued as the lift stopped and two junior nurses entered just as she strode out. She laughed inwardly, wondering, *what kind of a person treats me the way he did and then shows false concern? Hateful man!*

When she returned home that evening she had a phone call from her mother who had undergone angioplasty and was well now, but found out that her uncle needed another operation. That meant her parents' return would be delayed again, but she decided not to burden them with her worries and so painted a very rosy picture of her job, and shared her dreams of opening her own hospital in Dalhousie.

The next day she got her blood tests done and took leave for a few hours to give an audition at the Shimla Channel. In the afternoon there was a knock at her office door, and Karuna entered. "Where have you been since morning?"

"Why? What's the matter?"

"We were in the lounge when Dr Sarina rang up and asked for you to make sure you get all your tests done."

"I know about that. Dr Sharma gave me the first injection to control my low blood sugar. However, he insisted I get admitted, so I agreed to do so this Saturday."

"Oh," then her voice became excited. "Well, someone called Ravinder Singh also called for you. He wanted you to know he is staying at the Cecil Hotel. I just found out from Dr Mathur that he is the son of the ex-ruler of Pratap Garh in Madhya Pradesh!"

"Yes, I know, he was one year senior to me in Delhi. After finishing medicine he joining the IFS, and the last I heard of him, he was posted in Canada."

"Krina, can I ask you something?" Karuna said. "After Dr Mathur left, the chief stayed and asked me what was wrong with you. So I told him how you fell ill and the high dosage of floxacillin antibiotics affected your liver. Do you know what he said?"

"I'm not interested," Krina said, picking up some papers from her desk.

"He said you were stupid to take such a risk," Karuna continued. "He left the lounge but to tell you the truth, he seemed very upset."

"So?" Krina asked defensively.

"So...is there something going on?" Karuna asked.

"No," Krina said firmly, but Karuna eyed her with suspicion so she said, "anyway, I must finish my work and then go meet my friend Ravinder."

"What about your sugar levels?"

"Dr Sharma has told me to take more sugar to keep my level normal, but I also need one injection in the morning and another in the evening. I'm sure this is just a temporary phase and that I will be all right soon." She saw Karuna out and headed towards the lift herself. The doors opened to reveal Karan standing inside. Krina hesitated but he said, "Come in," so she did.

"Krina, you have to talk to me." When she didn't reply, he commanded, "Look at me!" Krina still refused. "You're not only stupid and stubborn but I must commend you on your knowledge of torturing people. I don't think you have any idea what you're doing to both of us!"

When Krina still offered no reply, he yelled, "You make me so mad I feel like killing you!" The doors opened at her floor and she stepped out.

When she finished her work she left the hospital and asked Bhola Ram the driver to take her to Mall Road. She handed him her shopping list but remained in the car. Realising it would be a long wait she got out of the car and found a phone booth to call Ravinder.

When Bhola Ram came back she asked him, "What took you so long?"

"I met Karan sahib at the shop and he stopped me to ask about you. I told him about your health and when he asked me why I was buying so much chocolate, I told him you had started eating a lot of it. He didn't say anything but just left with some madam who was with him."

She shut her eyes and rested her head against the headrest and told him to drive to the Cecil. *Why is he acting as though he is bothered about me when he's the one who insisted there is nothing between us?* She wondered. The only thing she had to hold on to was her resolve to remain aloof and not let him affect her.

# Chapter 9

The phone in Krina's office rang one day. "Krina, where have you been?" came sister Negi's voice. "We have a problem. There is an operation scheduled that Dr Kumar is to perform, which was initially to be aided by Dr Mathur. However, Dr Mathur has to appear in court for a family case and you will have to take his place. Now please be careful, we don't want a conflict."

"A conflict? Why would you think there would be a conflict? I haven't so much as even spoken to Dr Kumar."

"Do you remember the Kanti Devi case? The patient who is scheduled for a left colectomy? You requested for an extra unit of blood."

"Yes…"

"Well, Dr Kumar reviewed the file and he has cancelled your request."

"What?" Krina burst out, enraged, "how can he do that? She's sixty-five years old and her haemoglobin count is only 910!"

"I know. That is why I'm warning you, Krina, don't do anything that might create a problem. Do not bring your differences into that operation theatre. You are the only one in Dr Mathur's absence who is capable of doing this and he has left directions with me to convey the same to you."

"All right," Krina sighed, wishing she didn't have to work with Karan. *Why is he picking on me? First he corners me in the lift, and now he's openly humiliating me by disregarding my professional opinion!* In her frustration she forgot to have her morning dose of sugar or even put chocolates in her pocket as Dr Sharma had advised her.

Her mood was still stormy even when Neelam greeted her outside the operation theatre. Krina wordlessly took the patient's file. The boy was already on the operating table and her junior, Dr Sidharth, was preparing to anaesthetise him. In Karan's bold handwriting in the file was written: *The child is allergic to floxacillin*. Some of her anger faded away because she did admire him for being so meticulous and concerned about his patients.

She took a deep breath and recalled sister Negi's advice to leave her differences outside the theatre. So what if Karan had insulted her on his very first day at the hospital? So what if he had kept it a secret that the hospital she would be working at was run by his family? None of that mattered any more; the only task to concentrate on was the operation. Her professional reputation was at stake.

Neelam said, "He is being scrubbed, so get ready." Krina went into the changing room and changed into her gown and gloves. When she re-emerged, everyone including Karan was ready, but he looked at her in distaste. "Why has there been a sudden change in the anaesthetic team?" Kamlesh explained the situation to him, and he accepted it without a word. Instead, he entered the theatre and started working.

There was complete silence, only broken occasionally when he asked for different surgical instruments. Krina had to admire his skill and was in complete agreement with Dr Mathur on his competence.

While working on the anaesthetic form, she suddenly felt light-headed. She tried to take deep breaths and continued with her work, but soon the room began to spin before her eyes, and she felt herself losing her balance. Then she remembered not having taken any sugar so she dug into her pockets but they were empty. Karan had just opened the peritoneum, and she ensured that the patient was fully relaxed. She was sure Dr Sidharth could handle the patient for a few minutes while she rushed to get some sugar. She whispered to him to take control and dashed to the lounge where she stuffed a few sugar cubes in her mouth and ran back to the operation theatre.

When she returned, however, Karan was in an uproar and Sidharth was cowering as he fumbled with the controls. Karan yelled at her while she took the controls from Sidharth and increased the gas as the patient had begun to stir. "You're the senior anaesthetist Dr Mathur recommended?" Karan demanded. "How can you leave the theatre in the middle of an operation? It was not only an unprofessional thing to do, but also stupid, irresponsible and it makes you completely unreliable! How could you even think of leaving the patient when I was working so deep in the abdomen? Where did you go?" he was absolutely livid, "did you think you'd take a short break and get some fresh air? How could you leave your junior in charge? If he could do your job, we wouldn't have any use for you!" The harangue continued and Krina tried turning a deaf ear while she adjusted the gas levels. When the patient was fully relaxed, she finally looked up and said, "Sir, I am very sorry. You can continue now."

"Oh can we, now?" Karan's voice was dripping with sarcasm. "Have you finally found some time to attend to your duties?"

"Sir, it's just that sometimes a patient needs more gas than advocated," Krina said, ignoring him.

"And were you there to take that call?" Karan snapped. "Where the hell did you go?"

"I'm sorry sir, we can continue with my explanations later, the patient is ready to be operated on again."

Karan narrowed his eyes. "Pull this again and you will find yourself without a job." Silence reigned again as he started working and removed the patient's appendix. "Relax the patient more; I'm closing!" Karan barked at her. Krina didn't reply. In a fit of anger Karan threw the instrument on the floor and yelled, "Did you not hear me? I said relax the patient!"

"I heard you perfectly well, sir. It's just that the gas needs a moment." He glared at her as he waited and then she said, "Ready." As Karan closed the first layer, she turned to her anaesthetic file and began writing the report. Karan asked Kamlesh to close the rest of the layers but before leaving the theatre, he hissed at Krina, "If this ever happens again, I swear I'll make sure you never find a job in a hospital in India."

There was silence for a moment after he left, which was broken by Neelam. "Where did you go, Krina?" she asked, "Dr Kumar completely lost his temper and poor Sidharth was so frazzled by the firing he got that he couldn't do anything properly."

"I'm sorry, but Dr Kumar is arrogant and a bully. Sidharth, please accept my apologies." She went to the lounge and loaded her coffee with sugar again so there would be no chance of feeling dizzy during the next operation.

The only other person in the lounge was Karan, who looked at her cup and asked, "When did you start taking so much sugar?" When she didn't reply, he lost his temper again and said, "I'm talking to you!" She still didn't reply and he burst out, "Why won't you tell me what's wrong with you?" They heard footsteps approaching the lounge and Karan hissed in her ear before moving away, "I'm going to make you regret this."

They found themselves together again in the operation theatre for the next case. She first intubated the patient and then looked at the file only to discover Karan had scratched out her orders as to how much blood was required, and written his own. In keeping with his character, he insulted her publicly saying, "Do not ever leave an operation theatre without my permission." On getting no answer from her, he continued, "Madam anaesthetist, have you not been taught the rules? You are answerable to the operating surgeon, so don't pretend to be deaf and dumb!"

*God, I wish I didn't have to work with him!* Krina thought. *This is only the beginning.* Karan did his work perfectly, with only a minimal loss of blood. He finished up the entire operation in about forty minutes and left. Once they were all outside, Neelam said to Krina, "Why didn't you reply to him?"

"He's a bully. What's the point of replying?"

"If I had been in your place, I'd have walked out the moment he started talking to me like that."

Krina looked around furtively. "Don't say that, he might hear you." They went to the lounge where they found Karan talking to Dr Mathur and neither of them looked happy. Krina quickly made coffee for herself and was about to escape to the changing room when Dr Mathur said that he would like to have a word with her. She sighed and took the seat he gestured towards. Karan's lips were tightly pressed, and he left as she sat down.

"Krina, what happened in surgery that made Dr Kumar so angry?" he asked tiredly. "He said you left the theatre and put Sidharth in charge, and in your absence the patient moved and Sidharth was not able to control it. Is this true?"

Krina's eyes became downcast and she said, "Yes, it is true and I'm ashamed of myself, but it's just that I had forgotten to have sugar in the morning and I was so dizzy I could hardly stand. So I ran to the lounge to eat some sugar."

"Dizzy? Since when has this been going on?" he was very concerned.

"My blood test showed that my blood sugar has dipped too low and I've started having dizzy spells."

"Why didn't you tell Dr Kumar that?" Krina made no reply, so Dr Mathur continued, "Krina, Sidharth is good, but he doesn't have your experience. And what is this about you being too arrogant to communicate with the operating surgeon?"

"He said that?"

"Yes. Can I ask you something, between just the two of us?"

"Of course, sir."

"Is there some personal problem between the two of you?"

"No sir!" Krina replied quickly.

"I wonder, because even though he's a royal, I found him down-to-earth and kind, so I find his attitude towards you very strange. I'm sure if you explain your actions to him, he will understand."

"Sir, please, I request you, don't mention my problem to him. I don't need him to understand."

"I don't know if you can hide your problem from him because after all this is his hospital and sooner or later he will find out, but I do promise I won't be the one to tell him." He smiled. "I also promise I will try to ensure that the two of you don't work together unless it's absolutely necessary."

"Thank you, sir," she said sincerely.

As she was getting up, Dr Mathur suddenly said, "Oh, I heard you met Ravinder Singh!"

"Yes sir. He was senior to me, but I worked as his intern."

Dr Mathur smiled as well. "I know his family. Very pleasant people, most unlike other royals."

On her way to her office, a worried Sidharth stopped her and showed her the report of that morning's operation where Karan had written that the senior anaesthetist was missing and the junior could not control the patient, leading to a potentially dangerous situation, and that the incident must be taken seriously. "Don't worry. You're not the one in trouble, I am," she said and walked off.

In her office she looked at the view from her bay window but it only depressed her; the clear sky, the floating clouds and the song of the mountain could not lift her spirits. Where was God when she needed him? She found herself crying softly. *How can one man affect my life so much?* A few minutes later she reapplied her makeup and not wishing to be alone, she went to see Dr Sharma. He asked her to get her blood tested again, and cautioned her that if her blood sugar levels were low she was to take more sugar but only after asking him.

In the lift, she encountered Karan again and he said in the same authoritative voice that he used to use in school, "Come in! What's the need for all this drama? What's wrong with you?"

Krina still held her tongue, determined not to give in to him.

He loomed closer, looking intimidating. "Talk, or I'll make you regret it."

But she was saved once again as the doors opened and a nurse stepped in. Her presence made Karan grow quiet but the air was thick with tension.

She got out on the floor the lab was on and had her blood tested. She went to the haematologist Dr Sarina's office to wait for the results. Sarina wasn't in, so she decided to wait, but Karan had seen her go in, because as she closed her eyes, his familiar voice asked a peon to find Dr Sarina and then demanded of her, "Can you tell me what the hell is wrong with you?" She was silent, and he slapped her hard across the cheek, leaving her too stunned to speak. "Talk or I will be savage," he growled. "Why can't you let me have some peace?" he hollered, but Sarina's hurried footsteps cut him off.

"Sorry to keep you waiting, sir," she said.

"Don't worry about it, I just came here to ask you something about the file of the patient we will be operating on tomorrow. It's just that the number of eosinophils was very high."

"Sir, the problem could be due to worms. Geeta has the stool test report."

"Well, the patient is the sister of a local legislator, so I request you to pay special attention to the case."

"Of course, sir," Sarina replied. "Would you like some coffee, sir?"

"No thank you. I have a meeting at Snowdown."

Just as he left, a technician came in and told Krina,"Ma'am, your levels are too low."

Still reeling from the slap, Krina could only say, "Just let Dr Sharma know." *Snowdown. That means he's gone to meet Shallu. If he's so in love with her, then why is he pretending to be so interested in me?*

Sarina said, "Krina? Are you all right? You're looking a little off."

"Nothing, just that my tests don't look good."

"No, what's really the matter?"

"What do you mean?" Krina feigned innocence.

Sarina put her hands on her waist. "Krina, please. This man is very qualified. The students trained abroad, especially at his college are like an encyclopaedia of medical knowledge – on hematology, bacteriology and management of all sorts of blood and fluid electrolyte problems – and yet he came to me on the pretext of asking a simple question about a stool test? It's a little difficult to digest. So tell me the real reason he was in my office."

Krina shrugged.

"Please! He was talking to me, but his eyes were on you! He even stood outside the door to hear what the technician said about your report."

"He did?"

"Yes. Now will you tell me what the matter is?"

"I told you. I'm sick, I'm very lonely because my parents are not in town, and to be honest, that sugary coffee I drink is making me even sicker! If you want to still investigate my life, please feel free!"

Sarina laughed. "Fine, fine, I'm sorry. It's just the way he looked at you that I became curious." She poured some coffee for them both. "What a handsome young prince. Just the stuff of fairy tales," she chuckled.

"I think you don't know that he's engaged to a doctor at Snowdown."

Sarina was genuinely surprised but she studied Krina carefully as they both sipped their coffees.

"What?" Krina asked.

"You're tall and beautiful. You have a charming face and such an unassuming personality…all in all, you're so different, definitely better than any doctor at Snowdown. Who knows, maybe *someone* might be interested in you," Sarina said suggestively and said quickly before Krina could protest, "my husband saw you riding the other day and told me how good you looked in Jodhpurs."

"Now that you've had your fun can you ring up Dr Sharma and ask his opinion on my tests?"

"There's no need for that," said a voice behind her. Krina turned around to see Dr Sharma at the door. "Krina," he said seriously, "you need to get admitted for blood transfusion. Till then, you need injections administered twice every day."

She promised him she'd admit herself soon. As she left the lab the ring on her finger caught the light in the hallway making her suddenly stop and wonder whether the ring was the reason Karan was still pursuing her. He had said that it was meant for the person he would marry, and maybe he wanted it back, but didn't know how to ask. Convincing herself that it was the reason, she took advantage of the fact that he was out and decided to quietly let herself into his office and leave the ring there. Back in her own office she pulled the ring off her finger.

Her vision was immediately clouded with tears. She twirled the band for a minute and looked at it ruefully, but then decided that she had to be strong. *He's gone too far now; he slapped me. We aren't kids any more. He doesn't hesitate to insult me in public and I'm sure he'll bring up the topic of my disappearance from the theatre at tomorrow's meeting.* Squaring her shoulders, she wiped her tears, hunted for an envelope and slipped the ring inside.

She went to the 5th floor and found his office empty except for the janitor who was dusting. She entered his office for only the second time since she had arrived at the hospital, and for a moment, she lost herself in its tasteful furnishing, its lush carpet and curtains, and the turquoise colour, his favourite. There was a framed picture above the fireplace that she went over to peer closely at, and was surprised to see whom it was of. It was a blown-up version of the picture that Karan had told her he had of hers. She saw herself looking surprised behind a pine tree and Karan standing victorious over her holding the reins of his horse.

She felt extremely confused. If he really didn't care about her any more and was getting married to someone else, why was he giving out mixed signals? Why was he always cornering her to find out what was wrong and hanging up pictures of her when he humiliated her publicly and raised questions about her professionalism? She felt strongly temped to just confront him and ask him outright what he wanted but then she remembered the slap he'd given her in Sarina's office. *I will not entertain any more attempts to invade my privacy or any other sort of retaliation; you will only end up harming yourself. I assure you that your personal future is no concern of mine*, he'd written in his letter.

Those simple but hurtful words helped her make up her mind and she set down the envelope with an air of finality. It made her feel slightly better though the bitterness returned. At least now she could tell herself that she had no past with Karan and that she must move on.

Just as she reached home she received a call from the hospital that an emergency case had come up, a child with a blunt trauma to the abdomen, which required an urgent operation. Karan was already on his way, so they requested Krina to hurry. She was not looking forward to performing surgery with him again but she had no choice.

There had been an accident on the main road outside her house that caused a terrible traffic jam where she waited for over half an hour before the police officer she had told about her emergency got back to her and took her to the hospital in his own jeep. She dreaded Karan's reaction to her being late but had to face it silently, even if it only provoked him further.

The child was on the hospital bed. Kamlesh had just put a second drip, Sidharth was holding an oxygen mask over his face, and Karan was sitting by the boy, waiting. None of them noticed her come in and Karan asked Kamlesh, "So, madam anaesthetist cannot be contacted?"

"No, sir," she replied. "She's already left home, but she isn't here yet."

"I hope she didn't stop for some quick shopping before the operation," he said sarcastically but looked extremely tense.

Sidharth was the first to spot her. "Madam!" he said, relieved.

"So you have come!" Karan retorted.

Krina ignored him and turned to Sidharth and said in a low voice, "Tell me about the patient."

Karan spoke instead. "The only hope is to operate on him immediately, but you probably can't appreciate that, being such a callous and irresponsible doctor."

Sidharth looked uncomfortable but Krina looked expectantly at him so he said, "The patient was involved in a car accident and admitted at a hospital in Solan but his condition deteriorated so much that he had to be transferred here."

"Can I ask you why you were late this time?" Karan spoke.

"What is the provisional diagnosis?" Krina ignored him again.

"Ruptured spleen and close trauma to the left kidney," Sidharth said, looking even more uncomfortable.

"All right," she said and selected the instruments necessary to intubate him. She increased the oxygen and checked the monitor to see the condition of his heart, lungs and blood pressure, then increased the rate of flow of the intravenous fluid.

Karan stood up. "Did you hear me, Dr Khanna?"

Krina faced him without fear. "Yes, I did, Dr Kumar," she said icily, and gave Sidharth a syringe to inject the patient with. She turned to her apparatus and began selecting the instruments she would need, and then fiddled with the knobs on the machine to increase the flow of the gas.

"Then why don't you reply?" Karan almost yelled. "It seems you think you are not accountable to the chief of surgery! You have really stretched my patience to its limit!"

Krina couldn't control herself. "Tell me, sir, what can I do except apologise? My delay was not my fault. This child is in a poor condition and he is now ready to be operated on, so if you are done with me, you can begin your work."

Karan came close to her looking thunderous. "I don't appreciate your attitude, Dr Khanna. Do not forget whom you're talking to." He looked at her threateningly and left the room to go to the operation theatre.

She heaved a sigh of relief, confirmed the patient's condition once more and then had him moved to the operation theatre.

Karuna entered with the trolley of instruments and whispered to Krina, "Dr Kumar is really angry. Where were you?"

"Shopping," Krina said sarcastically.

"Krina," Karuna pleaded. "What is going on? The moment he looks at you he sees red."

"I probably irritate his system. He must be allergic to me." This produced a chuckle from Karuna. They became silent as Karan walked in with Kamlesh. Krina nodded at her, motioning to clean and drape the patient.

Karan took his place. "Can I start?"

"Yes sir," Krina replied.

"Thank you." The theatre was again completely silent as he worked till he said, "I'm now opening the peritoneal cavity as it's full of blood, so increase the rate of infusion of blood." She did so, but he kept looking at her expectantly. "Madam anaesthetist, when I ask for something, I need to hear you acknowledge it. God, how you irritate me!" At the mention of irritation, Karuna let out an involuntary chuckle but was immediately checked by the look Karan shot her. "Is something amusing you, sister?"

"No sir," Karuna said meekly.

"Then please concentrate on your work and keep the suction ready!" he ordered. As he opened the cavity there was a lot of blood, so Krina began pushing more blood to maintain the pressure. A few minutes later he asked for a vascular clamp and looking at Kamlesh said, "We cannot save the spleen; we have to perform a splenoctomy." He turned to Krina. "Relax the abdomen."

"But sir, it's already relaxed," Krina replied.

"I'm not asking for your opinion, Dr Khanna, I am giving you an order. Relax it more." With clenched teeth she did so and he removed the spleen. "Sister Karuna, ask one of the junior nurses to wipe my forehead."

Karuna was busy herself with the suction, so she whispered to Krina, "She's gone down to get another unit of blood, so can you do it?"

Krina wiped his forehead with the swab and for the first time he looked at her without anger or hatred in his eyes, but looked away without thanking her. "We are now closing the patient," he announced. "He is now stable." Krina relaxed the patient and Karan asked Karuna for the suture to stitch the patient up with.

"Please give the drug a moment to act, sir," Krina said. He didn't reply but held the needle and waited. "Ready, sir," Krina informed him.

He closed the first layer and asked Kamlesh to do the rest and left the theatre. Krina breathed in relief and noted the difference in the atmosphere when she worked with Karan and when she worked with Dr Varma. She also noticed the difference in Karan himself. He was quieter and had lost his fun-loving attitude. She wondered what the reason could be, since he was in a relationship he had obviously chosen himself. She shut her eyes as she realised that she still loved him despite everything that had passed. Feeling that way was very unhealthy. Neither of them could stand being around the other and their personal lives were getting in the way of their professional ones, which could only adversely affect them both. Krina was close to being convinced that she should resign.

Karan returned and asked Kamlesh, "Doctor, how is the patient?"

"Stable and well."

"Good," he said. "The staff meeting tomorrow is at 10 am. Please be on time, everyone." He looked at Krina once and then left.

It was after hours and so she was sure there was no one in the surgeons' lounge when she went in to make herself a cup of coffee, the pain in her stomach gnawing at her because she hadn't eaten anything since that afternoon. However, Karan was inside, having changed into a silk shirt and a black coat and tie, making himself some coffee as well. He and Krina looked at each other wordlessly, and realised she couldn't ignore her low sugar any longer, gave up avoiding him and poured coffee for herself.

"Why are you bent on poisoning yourself?" he asked when she stirred in her sixth sugar cube. Krina as usual didn't reply so he said, "I'll find out soon enough. Let me warn you, this will adversely affect your health, and this attitude you're keeping up, avoiding me, refusing to speak to me..." he waited, but Krina looked pointedly at the floor and drank her coffee. Then with a sneer he said, "Why don't you finish this one so I can make you another with *ten* cubes? That will get you to your end faster."

Kamlesh entered and Krina was thankful for the distraction. "Sir, Dr Shallu called to say that she is waiting for you at your house, and that you're getting late for dinner."

"Thank you, doctor. If there are any more emergencies, I will be at my house tonight, so you can call me there." He left.

At night when she reached home Krina was so tired she just wanted to go to sleep. She only remembered that it was her birthday when she saw the present from her parents. They had sent her flowers, a box of chocolates and heavy gold *kangans* with Jaipuri *meena kari*. Her eyes welled up as her nanny said, "I have been instructed to feed you *rabri*, so I made some."

"I'm not hungry," Krina managed to say and went into her bathroom to soak in the tub, still crying. It was her birthday and usually she would celebrate it with her parents but all that had happened that day was that Karan had insulted her. He called her a 'lousy anaesthetist', if Karuna had heard him correctly. *Pull this again and you will find yourself without a job*, he had warned. The following morning, he would insult her even more at the staff meeting.

She dressed herself and decided to go to bed without dinner. Instead, she had a glass of milk and a sleeping pill. Her nanny came to her room and said, "Karan called while you were in the bath. He asked me why you were taking so much sugar so I explained it to him. He told me not to worry and said that it would be all right."

Krina was silent for a moment but made no comment; she simply switched off the lights and went to sleep.

# Chapter 10

The sleeping pill made her feel fresh and calm even though the thought of seeing Karan made her nervous every day, but she was afraid she would become dependent on the pills if she took them too often. His blue Mercedes-Benz had just dropped him off at the porch and with a satisfied smile she looked at her finger where the ring used to be. She had begun erasing her past.

She had arrived early to get more tests done so she headed towards Sarina's office and found Dr Sharma there as well. He enquired about her dizzy spells and was relieved to know that they had reduced along with the headaches. He was confident that with time all would be well but it was imperative that she be admitted for blood transfusion because her haemoglobin was too low. He leaned back in his chair and said, "Yesterday the physicians had a meeting with Dr Kumar, and when it finished, he asked me how much sugar was given orally to patients with low blood sugar. I was surprised at his question and said that it depended on the level of blood sugar. So he explained that the other day he had seen an employee having six sugar cubes. I told him that taking so much sugar orally was enough to immediately raise very low sugar levels. He wanted to know the reason for transitory low sugar levels, so I told him that if the patient is not diabetic, then it could be because of drug toxicity or a liver disease, which is treated by being administered intravenous dextrose and oral intake of sugar."

Krina was silent.

"You know he was talking about you, don't you?" Dr Sharma said with raised eyebrows.

She hastily excused herself, not wanting to explain anything and hurried towards the conference room where the staff meeting was being held. She didn't want to endure any questions or be the subject of gossip in the hospital that she had by now more or less decided to leave. This resolve also gave her the strength to feel that she was prepared to face whatever Karan would throw at her at the meeting.

Slowly everyone began entering the hall and Krina took a seat next to sister Negi. There was a sudden hush when the door opened because everyone was expecting Dr Mathur or Karan, but to everyone's surprise, Shallu stepped in and quietly took a seat. Krina regarded her carefully. She clearly stood out as attractive, but seemed somewhat over-dressed in her fine jewellery and dressy clothes. Dr Mathur and Karan soon entered as well and the meeting began.

Krina was convinced that Karan would raise the issue of her being away from the operation theatre the previous day, and she definitely did not want Shallu to be present and enjoy her humiliation. She rose and said, "Dr Mathur, I am sorry to raise an objection, but I believe the object of this meeting is to discuss the internal functioning of the anaesthesia department, and technically it should not be open to outsiders." She looked pointedly at Shallu. "I understand that you would like to rebuke me and demand an explanation from me regarding the surgery yesterday and I am sorry. But I am not prepared to do so before an audience that has nothing to do with the internal functioning of this department."

All heads turned to look at Shallu who sat back with crossed arms and the expression of a person confident of her position. She knew that Karan would never ask her to leave.

Instead of Dr Mathur, Karan replied to show her who was in charge. "Dr Khanna, you are correct. I was not aware Dr Shallu was in this hall." Then he addressed Shallu directly. "Doctor, I think you are not aware that this meeting is only for members of the anaesthesia department of this hospital, Dr Mathur and myself. I regret to ask you to leave, but please oblige me."

Shallu looked completely offended and Krina knew then that she had made an enemy for life. The entire department waited for her to move, and finally, with narrowed eyes she said, "I came to see the architect incharge of building the new cardiology unit on the 6th floor but he was not in. It was not my intention to intrude but to watch how this hospital, of which I am going to be a part *soon,* conducts its meetings. However, if everyone is in agreement that I have no right to be here, I will leave immediately." She left the room red-faced and slammed the door shut behind her.

Everyone seemed to hold his or her breath till Karan who also looked displeased finally began to speak. He shot a look at Krina, "If there are no further objections, may we *please* begin this meeting?" There was no reply from her, so he continued. "This meeting, unlike Dr Khanna has alleged is not solely to persecute any one member of the team, but to discuss how to streamline the functioning of the entire department. Of course, that includes bringing members of the staff to task when they have failed to perform, but that is not the sole agenda." He looked around, "Today, I shall put forward my own ideas to improve the functioning of the department, especially where the installation of newer, modern equipment is concerned. I am open to suggestions and comments, as my aim is to make this the best hospital in the country.

"So first, I propose that we cut down the writing work of the anaesthetists. I do understand that it is cumbersome to be filling out reports and administering anaesthesia during surgery at the same time. I have already discussed the matter with Dr Mathur and sister Negi, and we are in agreement that a special recording system needs to be set up and attached to each department comprising added staff, answering machines and computers. That way, by the end of the day, everything related to the patients and anaesthesia will be available to the concerned doctor.

"Secondly, there will be a nurse who will be handed the charge of the anaesthetic department to lighten the load already on sister Negi, currently head nurse of surgery.

"Thirdly, mobile phones will be prohibited in the theatre but there will be someone to take messages for important calls and inform the doctor or nurse concerned.

"Finally, nurses will only be responsible for duties assigned to them by the head nurse or nurse in charge of the department, and will not be required to take on extra work. We will introduce technicians to take care of all labs and theatres.

"The final issue I want to raise is the one pre-empted by Dr Khanna, about her disappearance from the operation theatre yesterday. Dr Mathur is well versed with the details of the incident, and I request him to speak about it and give us his opinion and advice on how to avoid it in the future." He moved aside and took a seat.

Dr Mathur stepped up and gravely said, "There was an incident as you may already know, where Dr Khanna disappeared from the theatre during an operation for a few minutes and left Dr Sidharth to take charge. Well, I asked Dr Khanna about this, and she explained that she had a personal emergency and knew Dr Sidharth to be capable enough to handle the case. The problem only occurred when the patient became light and began to stir. Dr Sidharth, as I understand it, became confused and panicked when the surgeon, Dr Kumar, lost his cool. The fault as I see it lies at both doors. Dr Khanna should not have allowed such a situation to arise, but Dr Kumar should also have understood that during surgery a patient sometimes does become light. He should not have reacted the way he did, although we are going to make our best efforts to ensure this never happens again." He looked at Karan.

"If Dr Khanna had a personal emergency, is it not her duty to inform the surgeon operating?" Karan demanded.

All eyes turned to Krina, but she didn't defend herself.

"This is the problem, Dr Mathur! I encountered the same difficulty in the theatre several times yesterday. Dr Khanna does not believe in communication! Harmony between the surgeon and anaesthetist is essential during surgery. And may I add, yesterday there was an emergency case of a patient who needed immediate surgery and the anaesthetist who should have been there was an hour late. Madam, can you explain this?"

Krina felt indignant. "Sir, if you must know, I had hardly entered my house when I received the call. There was a traffic jam outside my house, on national highway 22, and it took me more than half an hour before the police could arrange some transport for me. If you do not believe my story, please ask inspector J. P. Singh who was kind enough to offer his own jeep to take me."

Karan shook his head at her. "Well, doctor, I had asked you for a reason but you had refused to give me one yesterday. Dr Mathur, this is what I mean about Dr Khanna's problem with communication."

The meeting continued and finally it was decided that a special staff car be deployed for such emergencies. Karan looked around and said, "Please, this is an open discussion, feel free to inform me of any problems anyone is facing." When no one raised any points, he said to sister Negi, "Sister, I'm sorry I denied you the pleasure of a small birthday tea in the surgeons' lounge. It is not advisable just yet as the new room next to this conference room will be ready next week."

The door opened and a peon entered carrying a tray with tea and snacks. Everyone began chatting but Krina slipped out of the hall and escaped to her office. She truly had made an enemy in Shallu, but she smiled cruelly when she thought of what kind of a temper and tantrums Karan would have to put up with for the rest of his life.

She was about to leave her office for coffee with Sarina when the phone rang and Karan's secretary informed her that he wanted to see her. "He didn't make an appointment with me," she challenged. "Please convey my regrets and let him know that I am very busy." She picked up her bag and moved towards the door when her phone rang again. It was the secretary again. "Sorry, madam, but sir says that he needs to leave Shimla by 2, so he does not have time to make an appointment. He wants to see you in his office at 1.30; it's urgent."

Irritated at his presumption, she said, "That's not my problem. Please let him know I can't make it."

Karan had picked up the line and told his secretary to hang up. "Stop making things difficult, Krina," he said curtly. "You *will* be in my office at 1.30. That is an order," he hung up.

Furious at having been put in that position, Krina stormed up to the lab looking forward to a confrontation with him and telling him once and for all to stop harassing her. She had also decided that she would hand in her resignation to him the next morning.

In the lab, Karuna asked her, "What's wrong? Why did you leave the meeting without even a cup of coffee?"

"I wasn't interested."

"Well, you know he had refused when we requested him yesterday to allow us to celebrate your birthday in the surgeons' lounge. He told sister Negi that he felt you were too unsociable. Do you know what she said? She defended you saying that you were the one who helped us get recognition in the Association of Nurses of Himachal Pradesh. She said that you were one of the most beloved doctors of this hospital and that any apparent unsociability was only due to your health."

"That's nice," Krina replied disinterestedly.

Karuna peered at her. "Everyone is asking questions. What is going on between you and Dr Kumar?"

"Nothing!" Krina snapped.

"What do you mean 'nothing'? Didn't you see Dr Mathur? Even he looked uncomfortable. You need to take this situation seriously; Dr Kumar is the chief of surgery!"

"It won't matter soon, I'm quitting," she muttered under her breath and left the lab to get more blood tests done.

It was past 1.30 when she finally went up to Karan's office. She raised her hand to knock but then hesitated, remembering the first time she ever went in and how he had insulted her. But she steeled herself and knocked. There was no reply so she waited a moment before opening the door and walked in.

Karan stood with his back to her gazing out of the window at the hills beyond. He seemed completely lost and didn't even notice her come in as she stood before his desk waiting for him to turn around.

When he still didn't, she coughed softly and he wheeled around. "Please have a seat," he said and took his own.

He was quiet for a moment, staring at her and then finally he spoke after deep reflection. "Can I ask you a question? Have you given a thought to your health?" She only fiddled with her hands in her lap and made no reply. "Don't you think that not only have you lost weight, you have become pale and sickly? I'd like to know why."

She looked straight at him and said cuttingly, "Sir, my personal appearance is not the concern of the chief of surgery, so can you please tell me the real reason you have called me here?"

Karan's jaw clenched. "Then tell me, do I have a right to ask you why you entered my office in my absence when I had explicitly told you that you did not have the permission to do so?"

She maintained her composure and said, "Yes sir, you have every right to ask me that. I admit to having come in though it was out of no reason but necessity, and I am not sorry in the least. I came in to place an envelope on your desk, which you must have found by now. And if you know what is inside that envelope, you would know that I could not have sent it with anyone else so I had to do it myself. As for why I did it in your absence, it was because I did not wish to be insulted and humiliated by you, as you are so fond of doing.

"There was a janitor dusting your office at the time and everything I did was seen by him. If you don't take my word perhaps you'll take his, and he will tell you that all I did was come in, place it on your desk and leave. I didn't take or move anything. I didn't touch any of your personal belongings or – "

"Did I accuse you of doing anything of the sort?" he thundered.

Her gaze did not waver, even though she could feel herself trembling inside. "Well, sir, those are the lengths it seems you can go to, to insult me."

There was a deathly silence.

Karan finally said, "You received my letter the day I joined. I explained to you in it that – "

"Frankly, the letter came too late, sir," she said bluntly. "You had already humiliated me in front of Dr Shallu and your secretary."

He ignored her. "In that letter I wrote that we must act like strangers and not bring our personal lives into our professional lives."

"Of course, sir, I have been abiding by the terms laid down in your letter. What hurt me to no end were the words that you thought I was trying to 'invade your privacy' or 'retaliate'. I wondered how little you thought of my character, how truthful you had been when you had claimed that you knew me and understood me. Tell me, have I ever given you reason to believe that I would stoop so low as to try and break up your new relationship?"

"Krina..."

"You're wrong, sir! Please, I advise you never to humiliate anyone to such an extent!" Now her voice began to break. "To think that...I can't believe I...for so many years I kept you at..." she stopped and tried to swallow the lump rising in her throat and to blink away her tears.

"Please go on," he said quietly.

When she had managed to compose herself, she began softly, "Ever since you sent me that letter, I stayed away from you and acted as though nothing was the matter. All you did was rebuke and insult me. You even called me 'lousy' at my work in front of my juniors! That was completely unwarranted on your part. It pained me but I've kept my silence all along. Why, I don't know! The hospital that I had begun to love turned into a nightmare for me ever since you arrived. I bore all your insults acting deaf and dumb, but there is a limit to how much I can tolerate, and yesterday you crossed all limits when you hit me! I figured it was the precious band on my finger that you wanted back, so I came and returned it," she said holding up her hand. There was a narrow strip of skin that stood out where the ring had been that hadn't been tanned. "You have your ring back, now please let me lead my remaining days in this hospital in peace. Please, let this be our final meeting, as I would like nothing more than to get every thought of you out of my mind. I agree that royalty must marry only royalty and I wish you all the best for your marriage. I was very young and foolish when I fell in love with you but I have learnt my lesson now; my parents were right about everything. Please believe me when I say that the lure of royalty never factored in what I felt for you."

He looked at her in silence.

"Though you have made it clear that it is no business of yours, know this: I am considering the proposal of the man I had told you about who refused to marry anyone but me. I promise you that I will leave and never enter your life again." She took a deep breath and smiled when she saw that she had stopped trembling completely.

Karan stared at her coldly. "You think that band was nothing more than a gold ring. How dare you take it off without my permission!"

She laughed, a little delirious. "Let's not play this game any more. It's all over."

"I hate you."

"Hate? That is usually what the loser feels in a situation, but here you are the winner. You've won. What more do you want?"

"God, you're so stupid and stubborn! You're deliberately trying to misunderstand me!" he shouted.

"How many more titles will you award me, sir?" Krina laughed again. "Monday morning you will see my resignation on your desk. I know full well all the financial formalities attached and I promise to pay the amount required to break the contract before its stipulated period. I am true to my word, sir. I may not be an aristocrat like you but I am a Khanna and I have some self-respect. You have stabbed me in the back far too badly for me to endure any more. It was only my love for you that let you take advantage of me so far, but I assure you it stops here." She stood up and made to leave. "Please accept my best wishes for the rest of your life."

"Stop!" he commanded.

She whirled around and stared angrily into his eyes. "Why?"

"Because I'm telling you to!"

"Oh, sir, you lost that right long ago," she said coldly. "I am not one of your servants that you can keep ordering around! I joined this hospital without knowing you owned it, and it was wrong of you to never let me know, either! I will not hold that against you, but let me tell you one thing: where your ensuring that I will not find any work in this country is concerned, please know that I perform my job with integrity and I, too, have friends and contacts who will never let me go unemployed because they believe in my merit. Goodbye, sir. I have nothing more to say to you." She spun around so quickly that she felt suddenly light-headed and she lost her balance. In her agitation she had forgotten to eat sugar again.

Karan swiftly caught her in his arms before she fell and made her sit down. He leaned close and said gently, "Krina…"

She looked at him, tired and confused. Then they suddenly heard the sound of footsteps and Karan sprang up and hurried to his own side of the desk. Shallu and her brother walked in without knocking. The major said, "Kumar, you're late. George is already in the car!"

Karan glanced at Krina and then said, "I'm sorry, I just need a few more minutes to clear up a problem with the anaesthetic department."

The major nodded and said, "All right, but the new development I needed to tell you about was that I've booked Shallu's room next to yours."

Shallu looked at Krina with burning hatred. "Oh, aren't you the famous Karuna Singh who insulted me this morning?" She turned to Karan. "Darling, I won't stand her presence once I start working here. We will just have to let her go."

Karan had the shame to looked embarrassed so to save him from having to explain anything, Krina said, "Dr Shallu, your wish has already been fulfilled. I am leaving this hospital at Dr Kumar's request. He clearly will do anything for you, so I wish the two of you all the best." She did not fail to notice the sudden glow of happiness that came over Shallu's face.

Shallu placed a kiss on his forehead and said, "We'll be waiting for you. Hurry." She and her brother left.

Krina was still dizzy from the lack of sugar but she tried to get up and leave as well.

"Krina, please, don't misunderstand me," Karan said to her.

Krina walked over to the door shakily and heard him get up from his chair as well. As she began to turn the doorknob, everything began to go black, and her knees buckled. Karan caught her again and his voice came to her as though from a distance, "Krina, darling, please…"

She pushed him off and with whatever remaining strength she had, she made it back to her own office, deaf and blind to everything till she took the required dosage of sugar.

There was a knock soon after and Karuna entered. "Krina, I saw you in the hallway, what happened? I called out to you but you didn't seem to hear!"

For the first time, she lost her resolve and burst into tears. "I don't know how long I'll live," she said a little too melodramatically. "I had two severe dizzy spells with such a splitting headache and they lasted longer than ever before. I almost fainted!"

Krina had knocked the phone off its cradle when she had searched wildly for her sugar cubes. Karuna picked it up and called Dr Sharma. She was shocked to find out that Karan was in Dr Sharma's office asking for Krina. "Krina, Dr Kumar is asking about you," Karuna said, confused, but Krina was in her bathroom washing her face. Karuna followed her. "He seemed worried about you." When Krina didn't reply, Karuna decided not to push her but just informed her that Dr Sharma was waiting for her in his office.

Krina assured Karuna that she was fit enough to make the trip herself. Karuna looked doubtful but left to attend to her duties. At the lift, Krina saw Karan again. He called out to her but she didn't respond. He placed a gentle hand on her arm and said, "Are you all right?"

She threw his hand off and said sharply, "Don't ever touch me again, Dr Kumar!" He sadly watched her get into the lift before the doors between them closed.

When she reached home that night, Karuna called to tell her that Karan had called to ask about her again. "Please, Krina, you must tell me what is going on! He seems very worried about you!"

She warned, "Karuna, I will, when the time is right. Please don't keep asking me about this. I just need some sleep right now," she said and hung up.

# Chapter 11

Krina entered the plastic theatre the next working day past 9am to find it unusually empty and quiet. "Where is everyone?" she asked the junior nurse setting up the instruments trolley.

"Madam, I was asked to tell you that this theatre has been reserved for Dr Smith who is to operate on Mr Prakash." When Krina looked confused, she said helpfully, "He came here earlier with Dr Kumar."

Perhaps Dr Smith was the 'George' that Shallu and her brother had referred to. Krina looked at her watch. She had received no instructions whether to work with Dr Smith or to find Dr Varma as scheduled, and the nurse simply shrugged. So Krina went to the surgeons' lounge to gulp down some coffee before the surgery, breathed in the fresh mountain air and got lost in the view from the bay window.

She saw before her the messy lawns that had become perfectly manicured, full of blooming flowers arranged in carefully designed flowerbeds, and the intermittent fountains. Beyond the hospital lawns she could see the city partially shrouded by mist but highlighted even more the beauty of the snow-capped Himalayas gleaming in the rays of the sun.

Shimla was so different from Dalhousie where the impenetrable fog wrapped the city till late afternoon. Though she would be glad to return to her hometown, sadness clutched at her at the thought of leaving the hospital. Memories of the good times with Karan almost brought tears to her eyes but she forced those thoughts aside. If she wanted to be free of the fear and dread of seeing Karan every day and being reminded constantly of what she had lost, it was a sacrifice she would have to make.

Someone softly cleared his throat behind her and she turned around, embarrassed. She saw Karan and a foreigner, presumably George Smith. He was lean and tall and all she could see of his features that were not obscured by his surgical mask and cap were his deep green eyes. She blushed as she realised he was smiling behind his mask.

"I was observing you," he said, amused. "You really were lost in your thoughts, weren't you? You really looked like a model posing for a sketch, and I wished I had my sketchbook on me!"

Karan did not look amused in the least. "George, meet Dr Khanna, our senior anaesthetist. Dr Khanna, this is Dr Smith, a friend of mine from New Zealand. He's a visiting plastic surgeon," he said formally.

Krina shook his hand and said, "I've visited New Zealand several times on vacation, to see my friends Margaret and her husband Paul."

"Nain and Paul Smith?" George asked, surprised.

"Yes, we called Margaret Nain. Do you know them?"

"What a small world! Paul's my brother! How have we never met before?" he laughed. "*You* are the Kriss Nain mentioned?"

"Kriss?" Karan asked with a raised eyebrow.

"Yes," Krina laughed at George. "They couldn't pronounce my name so they used to call me Kriss when I was in college in Australia."

"Nain told me that her friend Kriss lived in India and wished I could meet her." He looked her up and down. "She told me about you, but she forgot to mention how beautiful you are," he winked.

This exchange made Karan grow restless. "George, we came here to get some coffee before the surgery, remember?" he interrupted.

"Of course," George looked apologetically at Krina. "Perhaps we can spend some time together before I leave." They smiled at each other and George went over to the counter.

Karan, on the other hand, came closer to Krina and said, "Men find you irresistible, don't they?" he said sarcastically. Krina pursed her lips and looked away, but he grabbed her arm and spun her so she'd face him. "I've had enough of you pretending to be deaf and dumb since I left you at Jubbalhatti." He looked into her eyes but kept his voice down. "I've thought this through and now I am determined to face this storm head-on and live like a lion rather than a mouse under the constant fear that my blackmailer will strike and it will be my Krina who suffers for my family. We will be together at the end, you'll see."

George called out to him and Krina took that opportunity to hurry out of the door, her heart pounding, to her office. *My Krina. We will be together at the end, you'll see*. Karan's words rang in her ears, and she didn't know what to feel. There was such a conflict of emotions within her that she didn't know how to make sense of them. *He still loves me*, she thought, glowing.

The phone rang, bringing her back to reality and made her think, *but his words made no sense*. What blackmailer was he talking about? It seemed too far-fetched a story. Was it possible that it irked him that other men were showing an interest in her and he was trying to toy with her emotions for some twisted sense of pleasure? Memories of being constantly insulted and undermined by him at the hospital came back to her. She was sure this was some sort of new ploy to torture her, possibly even engineered by Shallu whom she knew wanted to humiliate Krina.

She answered the phone. It was Dr Mathur, who informed her that Karan wanted him to work with George and so Krina was assigned three general cases in theatre no. 3.

Krina was just getting up when the phone rang again and sister Negi said, "Dr Sarina was looking for you. Can you go and see her after your surgery?"

"Is something the matter?" Krina asked.

"Something about your blood test report."

Krina wondered what could be wrong as she reached the theatre but forgot about it when she saw the amused smile on Karuna's face. "What's so funny?"

"I've joined the club of 'lousy' professionals. I've been kicked out of my theatre, too, to make way for that foreigner."

Krina chuckled and they both caught sight of Karan who was not standing too far from them, discussing the case with Kamlesh. Karuna suppressed her laughter immediately, but Krina said, "Oh, who cares any more? Not I. I'll be as free as a bird soon."

Kamlesh walked over to them and said, "Dr Kumar would like to perform the appendix removal first."

"That's not possible because the boy ate some milk and bread only two hours ago. We'll have to do the other operation first and then his."

Kamlesh looked shifty. "Oh. Dr Kumar won't like to hear that."

"Just take my name. That should clear you from all blame," Krina smiled. "His anger will be directed at me."

Dr Rajnish and Kamlesh took care of the first operation, and when it was time for the appendix removal, Karuna came up to Krina and said, "Are you really leaving?"

"Yes, next week.

"But why?"

Krina looked over at where Karan was standing. "I feel suffocated," she said grimly. "I can't work in this environment.

"But I don't understand," Karuna continued. "He seems to be really concerned about you. He keeps asking about your health."

Krina chose not to reply, but went inside to have a look at the boy who was already on the table. She anaesthetised him and called for Karan and Kamlesh. When Karan walked in, she noticed something different about him. His manner towards her had changed. "May I?" he asked very politely, holding the knife above the boy.

Krina was surprised and replied with equal politeness, "Yes, sir." She wondered for a brief moment whether he had truly meant what he'd said that morning.

Karan worked without further comment till he had removed the appendix. The patient's parents were allowed to see the appendix before it was sent to the pathology department for examination. Then as he got ready to sew the patient he said to Krina, "Please relax the patient for closure of the abdomen."

Krina could hardly contain her surprise at his use of the word 'please' and looked up. He was looking at her expectantly but patiently.

"Sir, the drug needs another minute to work," she replied. "Please try now." Karan stitched the first layer, handed over the rest to Kamlesh, and left.

After the final minor surgery of an abscess on a foot, Krina stayed behind in the theatre to complete her report in the anaesthetic register when Karan came up behind her and said, "Why are you all alone here?" When she didn't reply, he said, "Is it just to avoid me? Krina, if you don't reply, I swear I'll do something we'll both regret. You know news spreads like wildfire in this hospital."

Sufficiently threatened and provoked, Krina faced him. "There is hardly anything to talk about, sir, we're perfect strangers."

"Krina, we're anything but strangers to each other! Didn't you hear anything I said this morning? Don't you understand?"

If he wanted to anger her, he had been successful. "Look, please understand something. I am *not* interested in your life or Shallu's. We may have had something in the past, but you destroyed all of that. And like I told you before, I am going to start a new life by settling down and marrying that gentleman you saw me with at the Clark Hotel."

His eyes blazing, Karan slapped her. Tears sprang to her eyes. "Say that again," he dared.

She raised her chin and tried to control the quiver in her voice. "You heard me. You have utterly destroyed my faith in you." She turned around to stalk out of the room but he clutched at her shoulder and pulled her back. "Why?" he said in a pained voice. "Why must we play this game when we both know we can't live without each other? Krina, look at me."

Krina continued to wriggle out of his grasp and said, "No. Please leave me!" But his hold only tightened.

"I hate to see you cry. Krina, you have no idea what I'm going through…I feel like I'm about to break!" She finally managed to escape from his grasp and ran off. "Please, Krina, wait!"

Krina locked herself in her office and gave in to her tears. She knew he was right, that she couldn't live without him. Kamlesh rang her up to tell her that the next patient was on the table and that they were all waiting for her. She washed her face and went to the theatre.

When they finished, Karuna told her that lunch was being served in the conference room in honour of George Smith. Krina made up the excuse of feeling sick so Karuna decided to skip lunch as well and have some coffee with Krina instead. They went to the lounge to get their cups where they found most of the surgeons sitting around George. By the time their coffees were ready, most of them had left and George was speaking only to Karan and Kamlesh.

Karuna said she'd wait in the changing room while Krina added sugar to her cup and didn't notice George come up behind her. "Wow! So much sugar! Are you trying to give yourself diabetes?" When she blushed he said to her, "Please let me sketch you some day. I know all plastic surgeons are supposed to be good artists, but Nain tells me I'm extraordinary," he grinned without reserve. "Now, what are you doing after lunch?"

"After lunch?"

"You see, our trip to Naldehra was beautiful but it was cut short. Karan had us all leave early in the morning on the last day."

"Early? How come?"

"Ask your chief," he said, bobbing his head in the direction of Karan who was listening to their conversation.

"I'll tell her when she needs to know," Karan said with a strange twinkle in his eyes.

George and he shared the most undecipherable look and George continued, "So what I need you to do is show me around Shimla and help me find some gifts to take back for Nain and Paul." Before Krina could speak, he said, "Do I need to take permission from your chief to borrow you?" He looked over at Karan. "Well?"

Kamlesh had also come up to them and said to George, "I have already made special arrangements with Dr Shallu to take you –"

"Next visit, sorry," George cut him off and looked at Karan again. "You will apologise to her on my behalf, won't you? Great! It's settled then. See you at 2 o'clock," he grinned at Krina, and walked away with Kamlesh, discussing the presentation he was going to make the following morning.

Karan looked at her and said, "You still won't talk to me, and won't tell me what's wrong with your health?" He caught hold of her wrist and hid it from view of George and Kamlesh. "I told you everything! Why won't you still speak to me?"

"Let me go," Krina said, keeping her voice down.

"You know me better than to expect that. If you don't tell me what's wrong, I'm going to kiss you in plain sight."

"You won't." Krina's eyes widened.

"Are you challenging me?" He moved closer.

"No!" Krina whispered.

"Good. Now you will come to the conference room at 1 o' clock for lunch and then Bahadur will drive you and George to the city."

"I don't want your car."

"You will do exactly as I say." She glared at him but finally acceded, and he smiled. "I love you," he whispered and let go of her wrist. "I wonder what so many people see in my ugly langur. The queue of men waiting for you seems to get longer every day," he laughed. He looked at her face adoringly and said, "I wish I could kiss you." But he turned and went to talk to George instead.

Back in her office Krina tried to wonder what had happened in Naldehra and what the look Karan and George had shared could mean, but all she could think about was how Karan had told her he loved her.

She received a call from Kamlesh saying that Karan's car would be ready to leave at 2. She recognised it as Karan's attempt at telling her that she wasn't to defy him. She made up her mind, however, that she wasn't going to give in to Karan so easily and allow herself to be hurt again.

Krina went to get her blood sugar tested and then remembered that Sarina had wanted to meet her. After giving a blood sample, she went to Sarina's office.

"You wanted to see me?"

"Yes. How are you?"

"Better. The headaches are not so severe, and the spells of dizziness are further apart." When Sarina nodded but grew quiet, Krina said, "Sarina, is something wrong? Something I can do for you?"

Sarina took a deep breath and told her, "Dr Kumar called this morning to ask why you were down at the lab so often, and if it's connected to you taking so much sugar. I didn't know what to do, he just cornered me, so I told him about your illness, and how you continued to take the antibiotics which led to drug toxicity in your system. I told him how you were constantly stressed, did not take adequate rest, joined a week earlier than Dr Sharma had allowed you to, over-exerted yourself, and have been delaying your blood transfusion. He asked me whether I agreed with him or not that it was dangerous for a doctor to be working under your circumstances, and I had to agree."

"Oh," was all Krina could say.

"But, the alarming part is what comes next. He told me he knew we had run scans on your lungs and brain, and he mentioned something about cancer. When I asked him what he meant, because everything appeared normal except for a small patch in the left lung, he told me to forget it, but rebuked me for allowing you to go on like this." She studied Krina carefully. "To be honest I was a little shaken up so I called Dr Sharma immediately and he decided that we would admit you on Saturday without fail under Dr Kumar's orders."

Krina listened to all this mutely.

"The only thing I'm happy about is that you haven't been taking your problem seriously enough till now, and finally there is someone even you can't defy. He even wants it in writing why we treated you without informing Dr Mathur and why we allowed you to work despite knowing your condition. It was a breach of protocol."

"Oh. I'm sorry."

"At least we can all be assured that our hospital is in Dr Kumar's capable hands, if he's taken so much trouble to investigate what is going on and taken the matter seriously."

When she continued to study Krina intently, Krina asked, "What are you looking at?"

"I'm wondering what is really going on between you two."

"Don't trouble yourself; there's nothing," Krina said. It was time for the staff lunch.

"Aren't you coming for lunch?" Sarina asked.

"No thanks, even the thought of food is making me sick."

"And the thought of our handsome, princely chief who seems so concerned about you?" Sarina teased and Krina blushed. "Hide it all you want, but I'm sure something is going on."

She parted from Sarina after getting her injection and decided to nap till she had to go out with George. She bolted the door of her office from inside and lay down. There was a knock on the door and even though she was awake, she didn't reply.

Thoughts of everyone's suspicion kept her awake. *What must they be thinking? Soon everyone will know about us.* Karan would not let her leave the hospital, she was sure of it. He had proven that when he held her several times in the same day with the full risk of someone seeing them.

Close to 2 o'clock she gave up trying to nap and went outside to the porch knowing that she had defied Karan's wishes of attending the lunch and would have to answer for it. George and Karan were both waiting for her and she apologised before either of them had a chance to speak.

George's and Karan's expressions could not be more different. One broke into a smile when he saw her and the other looked grim. "Krina, your shawl is just gorgeous! Don't tell me it's hand-embroidered!" George said, sensing the tension. "So did you have lunch? I didn't see you in the conference room.

She avoided Karan's eyes when he said to George, "I hope you enjoy your shopping spree, and maybe madam would join us for dinner at the Cecil." George climbed into the car and Karan escorted Krina slowly to the other side saying, "So you're bent on defying me. Just wait for George to leave. You know what I can do and there's no stopping me." They reached the door. "Have fun shopping, and think of me, because I am always thinking of you."

He gripped her arm a little too tightly as he opened the door and she gasped. "That hurts!"

"Yes, it does hurt when someone you love doesn't have faith in your love, and cares nothing for how worried you are when she pays no attention to her own health. Krina, you didn't even respect the sanctity of the blood I marked your *maang* with." He almost shoved her inside and leaned down. "Have fun, George," and stepped back from the car and returned to the building without another glance.

# Chapter 12

Krina was very quiet as the car left the hospital gates and let the realisation that Karan was not putting on an act to torment her anew, but that he was serious. He really did love her still.

A thousand questions sprang to her mind and to calm her pounding heart she looked out of the window trying to distract herself by spouting trivia about the city. She told George how the spelling of Shimla changed after the British rule and then told him about the genealogy of the city, how the Gurkhas called it Shyamala after the temple dedicated to the goddess more commonly known as Kali. It is said that it was a small village situated where a Muslim saint used to give water to thirsty travellers there.

The English discovered it in 1819 and Captain Charles Kennedy built the first home after three years, following which, the 12km crescent-shaped ridge became full of houses and mansions. The population increased once the railway connected it to Kalka in 1903, the same year that the British shifted the capital from Kolkata to Delhi, Shimla becoming the summer retreat, and the vice-regal lodge was built along with many other clubs and buildings. Entry to these places was restricted only to the English; the Indians were only allowed in to perform menial work. The British also brought polo and horse racing with them, which they enjoyed in the cool weather at Glen and Annandale respectively.

She looked out of the window and smiled. The car neared the Snowdown hospital and snaked through tall pines and oaks, and pointed at an old man sitting on a hilltop, playing the flute. "Can you hear the music and the women singing?" she asked George. "Pahari men and women sing these songs while collecting firewood. Life is hard for them, but one always sees them happy." Then she asked Bahadur to slow down and told George to roll down his window. "Breathe in the air."

He shut his eyes and said, "I can smell pine in the cool breeze."

She glowed with excitement and said, "Fresh from the high mountains. It is one of my favourite smells."

George clasped her hand and said, "I know now why Karan waited so long for you, though I must confess that I played a small role in helping him get back to reality." Krina looked puzzled so he continued, "My trips from Agra to Kashmir were all organised by Karan but he was surprised to see me having arrived early in Shimla. It was because of my mother's health that I have to cut my trip a little short. When he came to receive me though he portrayed a proud and perfectly calm disposition, I knew him well enough to understand that something was very wrong. He had grown too quiet, and I wondered why the girl he had talked so much about was not with him, but I kept silent because he did not broach the topic.

"He took me to his Thali house but was called to the hospital for an urgent case, so I was received by his father. I had never met him before, but he took an immediate liking to me and told me that someone was blackmailing Karan and had threatened to kill you. To get to the bottom of it, the detective agency his father had hired told Karan to play along and keep away from you for your own safety. But Karan was very worried about you, especially because of your sickness. Karan had never questioned his father's orders, but he was growing troubled. While we were talking, the butler entered to announce Shallu and her brother. I could see that Karan's father was surprised by their appearance but played the perfect host. She was not the girl whose photograph Karan had showed me, and she seemed to be grossly overacting, asking time and again why Karan was so late. When Karan finally did arrive, he looked tired and after everyone left I asked him when I was going to meet you. He told me we'll meet on Monday, and when I asked him why the delay as I was anxious to see you, he said he would explain at Naldehra. Since Karan was busy till late afternoon I provided company to a senior royal with whom I got along well. He told me the history of the Thali house and also about the anxiety hovering over it. He took me to Kufri and we had lunch at the beautiful Wildflower Hall.

"But the visit to Naldehra became a nightmare. Shallu forced her company on us, which came as a complete surprise to Karan, and with my help he decided he must teach her a lesson. She didn't allow the two of us to be alone together for an instant while she was awake. It was a wonder that he managed to sneak some calls to check up on your health. At night, though, the two of us shared a room and he told me the concern he felt for you and how he was so frustrated that he contemplated running away to Boston with you.

"I explained to him my belief in destiny, and told him about the girl I loved, Jane. She didn't love me, but chased after some rich businessman because of his wealth. It was my destiny not to be with her, and so I wasn't! So I told Karan that it was his destiny to be with you and he needed to fight for you.

"Shallu had made herself look beautiful only through plastic surgery. I showed Karan a scar at the back of her ear when she was drunk. Karan doesn't drink and I wanted to show him that she would stoop to any amount to get what she wants, and she wouldn't think twice about harming Krina. I told him that he needed to fight like a lion and that running away is no solution because he would leave behind his family to face the consequences.

"It seemed as though he had made up his mind because he woke me up very early the next morning and we drove straight back to Shimla where he took me to the hospital. In the lounge I saw a beautiful girl that I wanted to sketch but didn't know who she was, I still didn't understand when he introduced you as Dr Khanna, but when you left he asked me how I liked you," he winked. "The silly fellow wanted to test me!"

Krina listened incredulously.

George looked at her seriously. "Krina, he really does love you and everything he did was to save you from the threat to your life. After my surgery Karan's father called me up to ask how I liked the hospital and then casually asked about you," he smiled. "So I told him that he must marry the two of you soon before someone else steals you! He agreed and insisted that I stay longer. So I had to call up my mother in Auckland to see how she was doing. Nain is with her and my mother is very stubborn and strong-willed. I know she will get better soon. Nain had a good laugh when I told her about the incident this morning when I didn't recognise you and said I would like to sketch you."

The car pulled into the parking lot next to the city hospital, and getting out, Krina said to Bahadur, "You wait here; we'll be back in two hours."

"I'm sorry madam, but I can't," he said simply, handing her an envelope and locking the car. She opened it and found a letter and some chocolates. She unfolded the letter and read: *You're such a bother! Now let Bahadur accompany you, but it will be quite safe if you use the permit to drive in the mall. There is some sugary coffee in the flask if you need any.*

She looked up and saw Bahadur holding out a flask. Krina felt her heart flutter; Karan was so concerned about her. She forgot everything she had been through since he joined the hospital, because now she knew it had all been a lie. She smiled at Bahadur and said, "We will walk."

George, who had been photographing the hospital, walked back towards the car and gave Bahadur the camera. Explaining how to operate it, he stood close to Krina and the two of them posed for a picture. "I want to show Nain how well-maintained this hospital building left by the British is, even after sixty years of independence."

They walked to the market slowly with Bahadur close on their heels and reached the Tibetan market, the best place in Shimla to buy local handicrafts. Krina selected for Margaret and herself soft grass slippers called '*pullan*' in bold colours. George found a wooden pipe for Paul, and then caught sight of some woollen jackets that he went to try on. Krina looked through a selection of carved wooden boxes. She chose the one that had the three monkeys from the proverb, 'see no evil, hear no evil, speak no evil'. After scribbling a message for her friend on a piece of paper, she kept it inside the box and had it packed.

They made their purchases and stood at the entrance of the famous central ridge. Krina informed George that the ridge has seven peaks that encircled Shimla, and the best view was to be seen while walking. They were at the base of the Jakhu hill at the top of which is situated the temple of Lord Hanuman, where he was said to have taken respite from carrying the mountain from the Himalayas to Lanka when Lord Rama had asked for the *sanjeevani* herb to save the life of Rama's brother, Lakshmana, who had been injured while fighting.

They walked to Prospect Hill, which still retained its quiet colonial charm despite the crowded town. Around them stood proud, blue-grey snow-capped mountains. Those, along with the British architecture, set Shimla apart from every other Indian hill station. George pointed at a soldier with a gun and Krina explained that he was stationed to protect the national flag.

While he stopped to take pictures, Krina began feeling dizzy so she found a bench and sat down. Bahadur hurried to her and poured a cup of coffee from the flask that made her feel better immediately. Bahadur handed her a chocolate as well and regarded her suspiciously. "Don't walk, madam. I think I'd better bring the car; I have a permit to drive here."

"No, Bahadur, thank you, but I want George to enjoy the scenery. You know that the only way to do that is by walking. I'm fine, I promise." George sat down next to Krina, oblivious to her dizziness, so she told him, "In the summer, there is a huge festival that lasts a week where you can enjoy folk songs and dance. They allow horse riding at that time as well." She stood up and went close to a building with George and Bahadur in tow. "This is Christ Church, designed by Colonel J. T. Boileau in 1845. Rudyard Kipling's father, the principal of the famous Mayo School of Lahore, designed the frescoes here. Do you see that stain glass window there? It represents faith, hope, charity, fortitude, patience and humility, just the virtues taught to us at the school where Karan and I studied." She ignored the blush creeping to her cheeks at the mention of his name and continued, "It is said that it was here that Rudyard Kipling wrote *Kim*."

"Let me take a picture of you in front of the hills," George said, placing a soft kiss on her cheek. "I must say, you're the best guide I could ask for, and Karan is very, very lucky to have you." He took the picture and disappeared around the church to photograph it. Krina suddenly felt dizzy again, and Bahadur rushed to her with more coffee. George reappeared and asked, "Is something wrong?"

"No," Krina forced a smile. "Let's go to Mall now. There are no vehicles allowed there, so we'll have to continue walking. It joins the ridge at Scandal Point."

"Scandal Point?" George's ears perked up.

Krina grinned. "That was where the Maharaja of Patiala abducted the daughter of the British commander and so was refused entry into Shimla after that." In protest, he built his own palace at a new hill station which he called Chail.

George laughed and said mischievously, "Kriss, what would happen if I abducted you?"

"I'll have you behind bars!"

"Oh you can be so cruel," he joked. "But, do tell me about Chail."

She did, and then looked at her watch. "Now I'll take you to the Himachal emporium where you can buy shawls for women, and '*chaddars*' for men. They're like shawls, but larger."

After the emporium they walked on the main Mall road where Krina said, "There is a saying that if there is someone you want to meet in Shimla, come to Mall road, and you will find them. Everyone who lives in Shimla comes here."

"Really? So does that mean we can run into Karan here?"

"I don't know," Krina said, cheeks flushing. "It's just a saying of the locals."

George laughed and shook his head. "Oh, you two really do love each other, don't you? Wait till you hear more about what happened at Naldehra."

Krina hastily tried to change the topic. "Did you like Naldehra? Lord Curzon built the highest golf course there."

"Yes, we saw it. We even visited the Nag Nal temple. You should have seen Shallu; she was so tired that we had to help her walk 2 kilometres to a nearby village! The village was beautiful, but she was obviously not enjoying herself. What a woman."

Krina didn't like being reminded of Shallu and Karan together, but ignored the feeling and suggested they have ice cream as they continued on their way. "There was a famous club over which hung the sign, 'Dogs and Indians not allowed' on this road."

The sun had begun to set and Krina offered to show him Shimla by night. They stopped at the restaurant Devi-Co where they took a small table in a corner and ordered coffee. She slipped some money into the waiter's hand and said, "Can you open the balcony door? We'd like to go out and see the lights."

"You bribed him!" George said incredulously.

"It's acceptable in this part of the land," she smiled. "And if it makes you happy, then why not? After all, you're not just Karan's friend, but Nain's brother-in-law!"

Once on the balcony George held her hand and chuckled, "Karan must be home sulking with that woman, Shallu. You know, I asked Karan what I was supposed to call you once you two got married. He said '*bhabhi*'." Krina laughed at his pronunciation and tried to correct it. It was a beautifully clear night and they could see dots of light in the distance.

Once they left the restaurant and made their way down the road to reach the car, someone suddenly pulled her back as a motorcycle sped by and hit her on the leg. Krina collapsed and a crowd gathered around her. George helped her onto the steps of a nearby shop and the crowd closed in, making a commotion. "Madam, please stay here and I will be back with the car immediately," Bahadur said.

Krina was still a little shaken up as George tried to tell everyone to leave, that there was nothing to see. Bahadur was back very quickly with the car, and rushed Krina to the hospital. The wound was nothing too serious, just a minor laceration that a doctor bandaged and gave her a tetanus injection for.

It was getting late, so she told George to let Bahadur drop him to his hotel while she waited at the Shimla Channel's television station for her own driver to pick her up. Bahadur absolutely refused to leave her alone, and even George insisted he'd stay. "Look, dinner is at 8.30, so how about my sticking around for your audition and then we go for dinner together?"

She reluctantly agreed and told Bahadur to take them to the station where she introduced George to the director and went to change into a tribal costume. When she came out ready to begin the performance, she saw someone standing next to George with his back to her.

She didn't think anything of it and took the mike. "This song is about Lord Shiva and his wife Gauri, or Parvati, as sung by the mountain folk. Gauri was from a royal family and not used to a rough life, but she fell in love with Shiva who was a fakir who lived high in the mountains." She nodded at the musicians and then at the four other girls who sang with her. They sang:

Hun bho Kutanhi jo nachda Dhurua
(1) Bapua Lane terai oh lai
Hun bho Kutanhi Nachda Dhura
Bapua lanee terai oh lai.
(2) Ridia Tan Ridia Dhuru Mera Nachda
Nale, pule Gora Topdi.
Surinder rpt
Hun bho Ktanhai jo.........

…… ……………… Surinder
(3) Kutchia kunwaria babul da ghare
Kadhi to Bhiania Kadhi bho Chhadia.
Surinder
Hun bo Kutanhi………..

……………………..
(4) Gora Gora Hakan jo laganda.
Gora tan Hakan no Sundhi
Surinder
Hun bho Kutanhi………

……………………..
(5) Madva chalian chal mere Dhurua
Najak Paran Chhale wo Pandhe.
Surinder
Hun bo Kutanhi………….

………………………
(6) chhandhe chandhe Dhura Pani laianya
Najak latan nah bho chaldi
Surinder
Hun bo Kutanhi ………….

…………………………….
(7) Madia Dha Kura Madia Sutna
Nasa di beti Nasa jo Deni
S.
Hun………………..

……………………
Asa Bhulla Hunde Madia De jogi
Tun Tan Hundi Raja di Beti
Surinder
Hun bho Kutanhi………

……………………..
(8) Uchian Kailasha Shiv mera Basda
Hun bho galanda Gorana Basidi
Surinder

Hun bho Kutanhi……………..
. . . .. . .. . .. . .. . .. . .. . .. . .. . .. . .
Bapua lane tere
Bapua lane tere.
.. . . . .. . . oh lai.

The song ended and when she came out, George applauded. “What a beautiful voice you have! The song was beautifully done! I must have a CD of it.” He looked at the director, who very kindly arranged for one.

Krina blushed at the compliment and then caught a glimpse of the other man with George. He looked a lot like Karan, though now he was gone, so she couldn’t be sure. “I’m going home now. You should get back to your hotel, too,” she said and left the building after changing. Outside she cornered Bahadur and asked if he had called Karan and told him to come to the station, and Bahadur admitted the same without any guilt. “Now Bahadur, you know I am not well. My driver is here to pick me up, and I won’t be coming for dinner. I want you to let Karan know that.”

Bahadur looked worried and said, “Madam, that motorcycle that hit you wasn’t an accident, it was a serious attempt on your life. It was only because I happened to be extra cautious that I noticed him and pulled you back just in time. You might like to know that the police was alerted and that man has now been caught and arrested.”

“Oh?”

“Yes, madam. You know that I am a trusted servant of the family, and between you and me, I know that the drama with Shallu madam ended at Naldehra. Now Karan sahib and *bade* sahib are both very worried about you. Please, be very, very careful.”

# Chapter 13

The next morning Krina woke up when her nanny walked into her room drew the curtains apart, set the tea tray down and left. She sat up in bed rubbing her eyes and looked at the fog that had begun rolling in outside. If she wanted to reach the hospital with time to spare for a blood test, then she needed to leave soon. As she was getting off the bed she noticed that the picture of Karan was not on her pillow where she'd left it the previous night, but on the bedside table. She also noticed for the first time the faint smell of cologne.

She got dressed and jumped into the car with the nanny calling after her, saying she needed to talk to Krina, but Krina replied that she didn't have time, and told Bhola Ram to drive.

The fog was even thicker than she had imagined, and it took them more than double the time that it should have taken to reach, so she couldn't get her blood test done before George's presentation. She hurried to the auditorium and on the way was hailed by George and Karan. "Kriss!" George said with a big smile. "Feeling fine today? That's a beautiful dress you have on. Lovely colours."

Krina said with a smile, "I'll tell you the significance of these colours some other time. Good luck for the presentation."

Karan grinned slyly and said, "Krina, it's rude to not tell a guest in our country about our culture." He turned to George and said with twinkling eyes, "In India, there is a beautiful hill station called Dalhousie, where one animal is of particular interest, a species of monkey called 'langur'. The colours of that langur tell him apart from other monkeys, and those are the exact colours that Krina is wearing today."

"Really?" asked George, catching on.

"Really. However, one must beware, because that animal is very unfriendly and highly unpredictable. No matter how much you love it, or give it food, it'll scratch you. Oh, yes, I forgot! Krina is also from Dalhousie! So we must be careful, or she'll scratch us."

Krina made a face at him. "Very funny, Dr Kumar." She turned haughtily and entered the auditorium followed by the laughter of the two men, but inside, she was beaming. The sudden change in Karan gave her so much hope she could hardly contain her happiness. Her smile vanished, however, when she saw Shallu standing on stage looking well groomed in a red Punjabi wool dress with a matching Pashmina shawl.

Karuna waved to Krina and patted the empty seat next to her. "Where were you last night? I tried calling your house, but there was no answer," she asked when Krina sat down.

"I wasn't well, so I went off to sleep." She stiffened as Shallu took a seat next to her very deliberately. The overwhelmingly strong scent of her perfume made Krina's head spin.

Karan took the mike welcoming everyone and introduced Geroge, to whom he then handed over the mikes.

"Good morning, ladies and gentlemen," George began. "I promise I won't make this presentation too long, so let's start without any ado." The auditorium was plunged in darkness and the projector turned on. With the help of slides he talked about his experience in correcting facial defects, comparing before and after pictures.

Suddenly, a slide of him and Karan on ski slopes came up and the audience chuckled. "This was something Dr Kumar and I liked to do while studying in Boston," but then went on to explain how while visiting the ski resorts he had developed an interest in ski injuries and how it helped him in his experience to become a successful plastic surgeon. The house lights came back on and he invited the audience to ask questions. Someone asked him to speak a little on his country.

George laughed and spoke passionately about New Zealand and even had the lights switched off so he could show them some slides containing pictures, and compared it to India saying, "Our tribal cultures are also similar, so to speak. If anyone has seen our Maori tribes, you can see how much they are like the tribes you'd find here. Ours is not very old civilization, about 10,000 years of age. The original inhabitants are the Maori, who are much like the aborigines of Australia. It is believed that they arrived in this land from Polynesia about A.D. 1200 from the Polynesian Islands or Tahiti or Marquesos. These natives had no metals and no written language but their culture and spiritual life was rich and distinctive. They believed in their ancestors and various gods of land, forest and sea: Ranginal (sky father) and Papaluanuka (as earth mother). In New Zealand they have equal rights with the white race unlike in Austraila and they all in harmony."

He changed the slides to show his audience some interesting places to visit. "This is Rotorua, a sulphur-rich and dynamic thermal region with spurting geysers, steaming hot springs and exploding mud pools. It is a popular resort town with a Maori museum, temples and lakes around it. This next slide is of Auckland, our capital city, with two magnificent harbours, narrow isthmus punctuated by volcanic cones and surrounded by fertile farmland. It is close both to the Tasman Sea and the Pacific Ocean. It is also a starting point for treks to the rain forest, thermal springs, deserted beaches, wineries and wildlife reserves and the marinas. Our economy mainly depends upon dairy produce and tourism. Towards the south of this country cities like Christchurch and Dunedin offer views of beautiful lakes, snow-covered mountains, hills covered with grassy green foliage, flowers, tall trees, dense forests, and skiing resorts."

George ended his presentation with a slide of the Maori tribe in their colourful costumes dancing in front of a wood temple, just like many he had seen in India. "In fact, I was convinced of the similarity in our cultures when I saw Dr Khanna perform a tribal song yesterday. Both countries have such a rich history and culture. And though New Zealand is much smaller than your country, it is just as beautiful. If you think of our blue lakes, green valleys and snow-covered mountains, you are reminded of Kashmir, which I visited recently. Truly, when I was at Kashmir, I wondered whether it was paradise on earth, or whether New Zealand was."

The lights turned on again and Krina raised her hand. "Dr Khanna, if you'd please come up on stage," Karan said.

Krina got up and took the mike. "I have been to New Zealand, and it really is breathtaking, but Dr Smith, if you'd allow me, I'd like to say something about your dilemma regarding 'paradise on earth'. It is from something I wrote while I was in school, and I won't bore you with the whole poem, but I'll recite the last few lines."

"Please do!" George nodded enthusiastically.

Krina cleared her throat and said,

"Lay in bed, went to deep slumber,
Tolling of bells, opened my eyes
Across the mound, saw temple so white
Snow-clad peaks of mountain so high
Forest so dense, lake so deep
Valley so green and all in peace.

"Sacred flame behind which deity smiled
Within me I got my reply
'Life is short enjoy your stay
Nature young, youthful beauty ever green,
Paradise on earth where ever you stay
Where there no stress but peace prevail
In peace oh mortal you never debate'
Your paradise is in the land of birth it be yours till the last of breath."

She smiled at George. "My land of birth is my paradise." She handed the mike to Karan as the audience applauded.

"Dr Khanna, why don't you recite the entire poem for us?" Karan asked.

"Unfortunately, sir," she said, "I can't, because someone stole my diary and has not returned it till today." This caused Karan to blush a little, and Krina walked off the stage with a slightly smug expression.

"If there are no more questions, let us all break for tea," Karan said.

Krina noticed Shallu rise from her seat and hurry to the stage to talk to Karan and George. Karuna turned to Krina and said, "I'm convinced there's something between the chief and you."

"What?" Krina said, alarmed. "Why?"

"When you said that someone had stolen your diary, he turned red!"

"You're looking for something that isn't there." Krina avoided her gaze.

"Oh, there's no use talking to you," Karuna sighed. "Look at that Dr Shallu. See how she's trying to intrude on Dr Kumar's and Dr Smith's conversation. They are completely ignoring her," she suppressed a giggle. "I've noticed a change in Dr Kumar since he came back from his trip."

"How observant of you," Krina said and got up. "I need to get my blood test done now, if you don't mind." She was on her way to the lab when a hand clasped her shoulder. "Sarina!"

"That was a beautiful poem, Krina," she complimented. "But who stole your diary?"

"I don't know," Krina said evasively.

"I have a feeling I know."

"So now you're an astrologer, are you?"

Sarina laughed. "He couldn't take his eyes off you the whole time, you know. How long has this been going on? Anyway, there's no need for you to get a blood test done right now, I've already arranged for one at 6. See you in room 3. You're going to be admitted under Dr Sharma's care."

Sister Negi called out to her and said, "Come to the conference room, Krina!" So Krina fell in step with her. "I'm glad you're going to be admitted today. You need to get better. We missed you at dinner, but I heard you were unwell. Anyway, you didn't miss very much. It was a lavish but a very dull evening. Dr Shallu was dressed like a bride, with her brother and her cousin and they all strode in as though the event was being hosted by them."

"Negi!" Krina made the connection. "They're Negi too! Are you related?"

"We're distant relatives," the nurse nodded. "But they refuse to acknowledge me and that suits me just fine. I don't want to be associated with that family that was once royal but has now become one of penniless blackmailers and murderers!"

Krina gasped. "What?"

"I know they are somehow involved with the chief and are extorting money from him, except I don't know how or why. But the pressure he is under was clear from the day he joined, although I must say I have noticed a remarkable change in him since Dr Smith came."

Krina didn't say anything.

"Last night, I think they were planning to announce the engagement of Dr Shallu to Dr Kumar, but then I saw a heated argument between her father, my uncle, and Raja Sahib when Dr Kumar left the hotel for some time. Then, although most people don't know this, the police arrived, and soon after, the Negi family left. Kamlesh's father is a senior police official, and according to him, there is a case against Dr Shallu's brother who tried to kill someone at the Mall on his bike yesterday."

"I heard that was a minor accident," Krina said weakly.

"That's not what Kamlesh said. The entire family is under suspicion now."

They reached the conference room and Dr Varma waved at Krina. "Just in time, adorable! The tea has almost finished!" He thrust a cup at her and said, "Now tell me how many sugars. Six? Seven?" he winked. "Today I'll give you as much sugar as you ask for; who knew there was so much talent in you? We had a poet amongst us and we didn't even know!" He put his arm around her and said, "Look, sister Negi is jealous of all the attention I'm giving you."

Sister Negi rolled her eyes at them and looked at Karan and

George who were very deep in conversation.

"I'm very afraid of Dr Smith," Dr Varma declared.

"Why?" Krina asked.

"The way Dr Kumar is talking to him and keeps praising him, it looks as if he'll never let him leave, and then what will become of me? My job will be snatched out of my hands!"

Krina and sister Negi both laughed.

"Kriss? Got time to say goodbye to me?" George said from behind her. She excused herself and went to talk to George. "I missed you at dinner." Then he dropped his voice and looked around mock-furtively. "I know who your diary thief is."

"You do?" Krina asked in mock-surprise.

"Yes. He said he's going to send me the rest of your poem by post," George winked. He pulled out his camera and gave it to sister Negi. "Can you take a picture of us, please?" he held Krina close. When the picture was clicked, he grinned at her, and called Karan over. As soon as Karan moved, Shallu set her cup down on the table and followed him. Krina took the camera from sister Negi and said, "Smile!" as Karan stood next to George, and just at the last moment, Shallu managed to squeeze herself into the frame. Karan looked furious. Krina laughed, and said to George, "So, you're leaving?"

"Yes," he took Krina's hand. "I enjoyed every moment I spent with you. I consider you a very dear friend, and I must say that you will make someone a very, very happy man one day." He kissed her cheek and whispered, "Is Karan looking jealous and murderous yet?" Krina chuckled and hugged him goodbye before going to her office.

Karan walked into her office a few minutes later when she was ready to leave, and bolted the door behind him. "Going home?" he asked.

She nodded.

"When will you stop trying to avoid me? Why are you still torturing me? Since my return from Naldehra, I have tried my best to let you know I love you and I will fight for you, but you're going on pushing me away!" He came closer and she felt her resolve quiver. "Don't you remember our time together at the Valley View Hotel?"

She nodded again, but did not reply.

He sighed in exasperation. "The day I came here and wrote that letter to you, you changed, forgetting everything we had felt for each other since school, and with no regard for what I had asked of you before I left for Mumbai!" He gripped her shoulders. "What had I asked you to do? Tell me!" he shook her.

"To have faith and trust in you."

"And did you, when you received that nasty letter I wrote to you? How could you not know me well enough to understand that it was a lie? That my hand had been forced?"

"Maybe you don't remember the letter, Karan," Krina finally said. "And the way you acted with that woman! The way you insulted me! How was I to know? How was I to know that everything you'd said to me earlier had not been a cruel joke?"

Karan let go of her and clenched his fists. "How could you have thought that the reason I followed you was to get that ring back? I was following you because I was out of my mind with worry about your health! It drove me so crazy that I actually hit you," he said, racked with guilt. "You don't know all that I had to endure to protect you." He came up to her again and gently lifted her hand. "I thought my heart had broken that day when I realised you had no faith in me."

Krina's voice broke as tears spilled down her cheeks. "I'm so sorry!"

There was a catch in Karan's own voice when he said, "You're so stubborn but I just can't resist you." He bent down and kissed her. "I'll always be only yours," he said. "Those outbursts that you called insults in the operation theatres were just out of the frustration I felt and the pressure I was under."

"I love you," she sniffled.

"I knew even when you were with that man at the Clark Hotel or posing for pictures with George that we belong only to each other. I can't live without you." He laughed. "I could hardly stay away, even last night."

"Last night?" Krina asked.

"Didn't your nanny tell you? I couldn't stand that awful dinner without you, so I left for a while and came to see you, but you were asleep with my picture next to you. I put it back on the table and bent down to kiss you. Your nanny who had let me in watched me like a hawk so I had to whisper in your ear, 'I am yours forever, and no one can separate us.'" He stroked her cheek. "Then you murmured in your sleep, 'I love you'. Back at the dinner George told me how lucky I was to have you, and I told him that something inside me warned me that it was time for him to leave." He looked at her very seriously. "Now everything is out in the open and I am afraid that the blackmailer will try to kill you again. That's why I'm leaving Ram Singh here to watch over you." Squeezing her hand he said, "Thank god you are getting admitted today. I will see you in room 3 at 6. But wait," he stopped. "I was mad at you!"

"Why?"

"How dare you take a picture of me with that awful woman?" Krina laughed and Karan went on, "It actually reminds me of something that happened in Naldehra."

"What happened?"

"It's too funny for words," he said, but was cut off by the ringing of the phone. "You take this call, I have to get back to my office anyway." He let himself out as Krina answered the phone.

After the call, she began feeling a little light-headed; so she lay down to take a short nap. She had drifted into a deep sleep, forgetting to bolt her door from inside after Karan left.

She didn't notice the door open, and only started to wake up when someone pulled her up. She opened her eyes and demanded, "Who are you?" but the masked man wearing a surgical gown and cap lunged at her. She screamed and tried to move, but someone pinned her down from the back and slashed her head with something sharp. An involuntary cry escaped her lips as she thought her head had split open. She felt blood trickle down her neck and face, and swam in a semi-conscious state, in too much agony to even try to move. She could do nothing but squeeze her eyes shut and think about the searing pain that was ripping through her head. A woman saying, "I'll meet you in the parking lot," was all she heard before she gave in and lost consciousness completely.

# Chapter 14

Krina opened her eyes to the sound of chirping birds and whispers all around her that said, "She's alert," and, "She's coming out of it." Her eyes couldn't adjust properly to the sunlight that spilled in through the window, and she wondered where she was, trying to orient herself. The ceiling most definitely did not look like her room, but it seemed familiar…

She tried to move her right hand but realised it was strapped and she was on a drip. She vaguely felt someone holding her left hand as she stirred, and she began swimming into unconsciousness as she heard, "Shh, darling, don't try to move…"

When she regained consciousness, it was no longer day, the sky was studded with stars and then saw moon coming out behind the white-clouds. She tried to move but there was something weighing her left hand down. She forced herself to be more alert, and finally realised she was in the hospital. She was still on a drip, but the weight on her left hand was Karan's head. It appeared that he'd fallen asleep on his chair. She looked at his sleeping head and smiled. She tried to wriggle her hand out from under him, and the movement made him wake up with a start. "Krina?"

The sight of his unshaven face filled her with relief and she smiled at him. "Karan."

He put a finger on her lips and said, "No, don't try to talk yet." His eyes were brimming with tears and he said, "I was so afraid." His concern spoke of tenderness and trust. He leaned over and placed a kiss on her forehead. "These last four days have been a nightmare for me! Look at how much you make me suffer!" He smiled. "Are you hungry?"

She nodded.

"Of course you are, you Pahari langur. You're always hungry." He kissed her on the mouth and then suddenly remembered that they were not alone and jerked back up.

Neelam was looking away uncomfortably, but she said, "I shall inform Dr David that she is conscious."

Karan laughed as she left the room and said to Krina, "The rules I set are being applied against me! David is your doctor, and I am just a visitor, not the chief of surgery." He looked at her with fresh tears. "This is the first time in four days I have even been able to smile; you had me so worried, I never left your side. You had the entire hospital gossiping about us. I think I heard someone call it a 'fairy tale romance'." He lifted her left hand up to let her see the ring that was back on her finger. "Now you had better not take this off again!"

"Sir, may I examine her?" Dr David's voice interrupted them.

"Of course, doctor," Karan got up to leave. "I'll be waiting outside."

Dr David watched him leave and then smiled at Krina. "Good to have you back." When he finished examining her, Karan strode in with a nurse who carried a tray of cornflakes and milk. She set the tray down on the table by the bed and asked Krina, "Ma'am, how much sugar?"

"Six," Karan winked.

"Two is enough, thank you," Krina said, and began eating. "How long was I unconscious?"

"There will be enough time for explanations later," Karan promised. "Right now, I just want you to rest and get better. Now that I know you're going to be fine, I think I can catch up on some much-needed sleep." He pressed the bell and Neelam entered. "Take care of her. If anything happens, I'm in the room next door." he said, and left.

Neelam looked at Krina sympathetically. "He has barely slept since we found you."

Krina felt a surge of emotion within her. After everything that had happened, she could clearly see their future together and it looked so bright that it filled her with warmth. She didn't know whether it was the medication or the fatigue, but she fell asleep again before she knew it.

The next time she awoke, it was morning again and the deep green Shimla hills greeted her. She could see the sky from the window only, which was mostly clear but some black clouds loomed in the horizon.

She turned her head and saw Karuna sitting in the chair next to her bed. "Good morning," she smiled.

"Karuna, what are you doing here?"

"Looking after you, of course. The prince has deputed me to look after you while he rests. Didn't I always say I knew there was something going on? Believe me, you didn't do a very good job trying to hide it."

Still too embarrassed to talk about it, Krina asked instead, "What happened? How did I end up here?"

"Well, you tell us!" Karuna exclaimed. "When I came to see you after lunch your door was half open. I came in and saw a cap and mask lying at the door and when I saw you lying on the floor in a pool of blood, I thought you were dead! I ran to get help, and Dr Mathur and his clerk came. We took you to the ICU and tried to resuscitate you. I really thought you weren't going to make it because even though you hadn't lost too much blood, your haemoglobin was so low that even a small amount of blood loss – of 600-1000 ml – could be fatal. There weren't enough units of your blood group, so Dr Varma, Neelam and I went to donate some. By the time we returned your blood pressure had come up but tachycardia was over 110 min, and you were still unconscious. Dr Kumar was not reachable and we were all panicking because your heart rate was too high. But it turned out that Ram Singh who was stationed outside the hospital informed Dr Kumar's father, Raja Sahib, and somehow Dr Kumar was contacted. Raja Sahib came immediately with two doctors from the Snowdown hospital and three nurses who all went inside the intensive care unit and arranged for more blood for you.

"Sister Negi called me inside to help Dr Ram Dass and Dr Gupta, a neuro-surgeon, from Snowdown, and I took my position with her and Neelam. They had finally managed to stop the bleeding, and your heart rate was back to normal. The entire ICU had been emptied for you and Raja Sahib was in a vacant room next to yours. He was very worried. Once you were resuscitated, the doctors discussed your history of past illnesses with Dr Sarina and Dr Sharma. Dr Sharma looked very guilty because he knew that he should have admitted you sooner because now the risk had increased. Raja Sahib told the doctors that they must do whatever they could to save you, even if they had to fly you to Delhi because you were too important to him and his son. Your head had been x-rayed and now we could only wait for the results. Your hemoglobin had gone down to 3.70, so you were given total six units of type B blood. The inspection of the wound was deferred to the next day and you were put on the critical list, diagnosed with blunt brain trauma with a deep puncture wound on the scalp.

"By now, the police had surrounded the hospital and Kamlesh's father, Inspector General of police Mr. S.P. Kalra, was in charge of the case. They found a surgical knife in your office aside from the cap and mask I had already seen. Your telephone wire had been cut, and the alarm button had also been removed. Everyone was talking about it, and Kamlesh told us how Dr Kumar had probably foreseen something like this happening, because before leaving he had given Kamlesh instructions that in case of any emergency regarding you, his father was to be contacted, and gave him Dr Smith's mobile number in case he himself was unreachable.

"Back in the ICU, Dr Gupta declared that you were stable and that there was nothing to worry about. The cut on your head was the cause of your unconsciousness and though deep was not at all fatal. The drug toxicity problem caused the anaemia leading to the oedema in the brain. It would be solved if you were kept on a cortisone drip and all you needed was some time to recover. He assured Raja Sahib that he would be there to look after you personally.

"Dr Kumar soon reached the hospital and though the ICU was filled with people, he only saw his father who placed a hand on his shoulder and led him to you. I must commend his ability to keep himself composed at a troubled time. He was perfectly calm, though we could see his eyes misted over, he did not let it reflect any other way. I knew for sure then that he loved you and I was in awe of such love, thinking of how lucky you were. Only when his father left, did he hold your hand. Everyone else had also been cleared out by now, and apart from him, only Kamlesh and I were in the room. He arranged the duties of the nurses from the army hospital and arranged for their stay, because the rest of the staff apart from Neelam and Mehra was to go back to their duties. He put those nurses on 6-hour shifts, the sheets were to be changed every 4 hours and there was always one doctor on duty to keep an eye on you. Raja Sahib was waiting in Dr Kumar's office, and so he left Dr Mathur to take over late at night. Neelam rang me up at about 12.30 at night to tell me that you had opened your eyes but only for a few seconds before you lost consciousness again. Dr Kumar sat there from morning till 6pm next day, and used the opportunity to place a gold band on your left finger and planted a kiss on it then covered it with a band-aid."

"I forgot it was Karan's birthday," Krina murmered.

Karuna continued, "The next day was a surprise because there were policemen in civilian clothing posted outside your room and sister Negi wasn't allowed inside. No one knows why. But the real surprise came when he asked to see me in his room. A room of the ICU had been temporarily converted into his private room, and had been done up like a five-star hotel. He was sitting on his sofa, waiting for me, and even offered me some coffee. I refused because

I was too scared; he had never asked to see me before.

"He had regained his royal composure entirely, and he said that he had found out I was very close to you, so he asked how we had got to be that way. I told him all about how when you joined this hospital, the nursing staff was debating whether to participate in the annual nursing event of Himachal Pradesh, and you had been so easy to talk to and so encouraging about it, how you organised to teach us a dance and help me prepare for the debating competition, both of which we won. I said that you became a beloved staff member very quickly not just among us nurses, but also with doctors like Dr Sarina. Then I told him about how you helped with my mother's operation in Delhi when we could see no light, and was amazed to know that you belonged to a wealthy family from Dalhousie. As the days passed you seemed to be bit sad and lost in day dreams, till Wing Commander Rajinder Singh joined the cantonment and we saw you going there to ride with him and eat dinner out. But he went to Leh and you stopped going out again. I also told him about our Kufri trip and how you came to try to rescue us when our car got stranded in the snowstorm that gave you pneumonia. I informed him about your nanny's worries that you were not eating, were having antibiotics and getting weaker. I also admitted to him that I saw a major change in you since he joined the hospital, and how you had been so stubborn regarding your illness and getting admitted, even after knowing that you had low haemoglobin and white cell count.

"Then, will you believe it, he told me that the two of you had met at school and had fallen in love! Krina, you don't realise how lucky you are to be so loved by him! I could see that he was very tired, so I offered to keep watch over you while he rested. He agreed and called Ram Singh to give me a special permit, which reminded me of how sister Negi hadn't been allowed to see you, which is very strange, but I'm sure he had good reason. Your room is constantly protected by the police and it was only yesterday that Dr Mathur told me who was behind the accident."

"He did?" Krina said breathlessly. "Who?"

"You'll have to ask him that yourself," Karuna smiled mysteriously. "Right now, you need to eat."

"But I'm not hungry!" she protested. "Tell me who it was!"

Karan entered and said, "So you're up! Good. Karuna, get me her file and two bottles of glucose saline, but please create a new access to her vein." He smiled at Krina. "It's perfectly fine if you don't want to eat."

Krina understood what he was doing. "Fine," she accepted defeat. "I would rather have food than those fluids you're ordering".

"Good," Karan said, victorious. He bent down to kiss her, and Karuna, red-faced escaped from the room to give them some privacy.

# Chapter 15

It had been ten days since the incident and being in the hospital as a patient had begun to irritate Krina. Not only did she feel too confined but she heard hushed whispers all around, tongues wagging about her and Karan, especially since he had announced that they'd all hear wedding bells soon.

She looked forward to being discharged and going back to her cottage and being under the care of her nanny rather than doctors, and have Karan hover around her without causing more rumours. She smiled at the thought of being alone with Karan without the entire hospital staff watching.

The morning that she was discharged, she felt a little weak but it was nothing like her spells of dizziness. She refused the wheelchair and walked down instead with Neelam. She wanted to see sister Negi who hadn't been granted permission at all to see her. Krina wondered whether the prohibition was because she shared the same surname as the Shallu and the major.

Waiting at the porch was a new white Mercedes-Benz. At first she thought it was Karan's but then Bahadur got out and opened the backseat door for her. Embarrassed at the fresh round of gossip this would bring about, she got in quickly, but Bahadur took his time in giving her a soft white rug to put over her knees and an envelope along with a single red rose. She waved at Neelam and looked at the envelope only once the car began moving.

She had expected the letter to be from Karan, but was surprised to see it was from his father.

*You don't know how important you are not only to Karan*

*but to me as well. Today as you leave this hospital, you are no longer my daughter-in-law, but my daughter.*

*This car is yours as a token of the love and appreciation of myself and my wife, and a welcome to the Thali house. I now anxiously look forward to the day you will bring back my first grandchild from the very same hospital.*

He signed the letter with his love and regards. Krina was very touched but wondered why he had called her his daughter-in-law when she Karan weren't married as yet. She put the letter in her handbag and watched the scenery roll past and rolled down the window to get a whiff of pine once again. The sun was shining and the sky was clear except those dark clouds that still loomed in the distance. This she did not take as an ill omen, but rather, thought that the weather could be so unpredictable. Rain to her signified a romantic atmosphere rather than anything else.

She listened to the chirping of the birds, the winter crow, the magpies, and the thrush with its melodious voice like a flute. After being confined to the hospital for so many days, she appreciated nature the liveliness of it, the colours, the sounds and the smells even more.

She watched the familiar Rampur Road draw closer but was surprised when Bahadur turned left instead. She was about to ask him where he was going, but then thought it might be one of Karan's schemes, and if there was one person Bahadur was loyal to, it was Karan. If Karan had asked him to keep silent about what was going on, no one could drag it out of him. So Krina just sat back and observed the route they were taking, constantly trying to guess where they might be going.

He turned the car to a road she knew well. It led to Mashobra, what had been a small weekend retreat for the viceroy because Shimla had begun becoming crowded. It was built by Lord Curzon in 1805 and houses the world's highest water lift still in use.

She watched the hill maidens pass by and remembered how Karan would scare them with his stallion. She couldn't help but smile at the thought that after a brief stormy period, Karan was back to his old self.

She gazed at the fallen flowers that carpeted the road in mauve, yellow, white and red. Deodars and oaks lined the road and she knew why Mashobra was such a popular retreat. Its beauty lay in the tall trees and green slopes, popular picnic spots.

"Every year there is a Sipi fair in late April," Bahadur said, noticing that she was looking around with keen interest. "It is a 2 kilometre walk to Sipur village where you'll find the most beautiful, old deodar tress. The villagers consider the trees sacred and say that they belong to a local deity, Seep, who can be identified as Shiva. Raja Sahib used to visit the animal fight which was always held at the temple in honour of the God Sipi."

She smiled at him and watched the scattered green tin roofed chimneys through the foliage, remnants of British architecture. The car drove up a steep hill and between the trees Krina could see clearings full of daffodils, hyacinths and other wild flowers.

"That temple at the top of the hill is of the Goddess Durga, centuries old. Bade Maharaj and Rani Sahiba would come here to pray."

Krina folded her hands in respect. Such a beautiful place, so close to Shimla was a treat to the eyes and filled her with happiness.

The beautiful Mashobra retreat was only 12km from Shimla, at a height of 2150m above sea level. Bahadur told her how the dense forests made it a very wet place with heavy snowfall in the winter, and how it was the hub of tourists during summer. The road suddenly became surrounded by shops but they were still shut, it being only 9.30 in the morning. Bahadur drove on and after turning right drove through a gate. The sign said they were at the civil courts. *Why has Karan brought me here?* She wondered. Could it be because hers was a medico-legal case? The car stopped and two men in the Thali uniform saluted, and she saw Karan come towards the car wearing a formal suit with a light blue shirt and red tie. He opened the door and said, "Cover your head with your scarf."

"But Karan –"

He put a finger on his lips and motioned for her to follow him. They climbed up the stairs closely followed by the guards as people stopped to watch them. They entered a narrow corridor of a courthouse, and she wondered whether this had anything to do with a case against the major, but in the room they entered sat a magistrate. He got up, greeted Karan and called for the witnesses. Ram Singh and another man Karan identified as Babit Singh from Thali came in. Fifteen minutes later, to Krina's surprise, she and Karan were declared husband and wife. Karan grinned and slipped on a gold ring on her finger, and handed her one to put on his. With a shy smile she did so, and signed the register.

They left the court together in the car Krina had come in, and Karan said to Bahadur, "To Thali house!" He took her hands and looked deep in her eyes and said, "To our house. Our house, of which I had no opportunity to talk to you since I came to Shimla."

"Our house?"

"Even George knows about our house, but I couldn't find the right time to tell you.

He laughed. "You're no longer Krina, but Mrs Karan Singh! I like the sound of that." He kissed her cheek. "It was my parents' idea to get a marriage licence. The last month has been so hard on us both, but now we're finally together, and nothing can tear us apart. When you were unconscious, I thought I had lost you and –" he stopped.

"Let's not talk of the past," she said, and changed the topic. "This place is beautiful!" she said looking out of the window. "Thank you for bringing me here."

"It gets a little crowded in summer but it still retains its sylvan charm," he smiled.

The car made its way back to Shimla, but to Krina's surprise, took the road to the hospital. When she asked Karan where they were going, he replied, "There are two approaches to our house." The car reached the hospital gate but instead of going in, turned right. "The second one is from the National Highway."

The path was wide and cemented, still flanked by trees, and the slope finally gave way to level ground. She could see the hospital and its lawns till they approached a gate that swung open. The house was as beautiful, if not more, than the one at Kasauli. Krina took it all in, in awe. As the car slowly went up the driveway, guards threw marigold flowers at the car and Bahadur drove around the central fountain which depicted a marble woman in a sari holding a pitcher from which flowed the water into a tank full of lotuses. They arrived at a palatial double storey house with a red tiled roof with chimneys, and towers at both ends.

Like in the house at Kasauli, the car stopped in front of a wide marble porch where Krina covered her head and greeted everyone who stood there to receive them. Together they climbed the stairs under a shower of rose petals and waited at the last step where the door opened and Karan's nanny stood on the other side. She performed the same ritual like she had at Kasauli and they entered the house. This house was even grander, with a Persian carpet on the floor, enormous chandeliers suspended from the ceiling, and the portraits of Karan's ancestors adorned these walls as well.

Karan led her to a hall where a portrait of him as a child with his grandparents hung above the fireplace. "That is my grandmother, Rani Padma Wati, after whom the hospital has been named." She was covered from head to toe in fine clothes and heavy diamond jewellery, and Karan, a little boy of two at the time, sat in her lap wearing equally exquisite clothes and a turban with a diamond and peacock feather. "And that is my grandfather." A distinguished man stood next to Karan and his grandmother, holding a sword.

"It's a beautiful portrait," Krina marvelled, and touched her head to their feet.

Karan put a hand on her shoulder and said with a grin, "And that is me. Look how handsome I was, even then."

"But just as naughty, even at the age of two," she teased.

He laughed and led her to the *puja* room where they entered barefoot.

The room was small and at one end sat a pundit and a black *dhatu* deity on a lion made of silver. Incense in silver containers and diyas were burning all around except for the one main diya on the gold stand.

He handed her a match. "Here. Light it."

"No," she said. "Either you go first or we do it together."

"That was a test," he smiled. "Come, let's light it together."

The pundit got up and performed the puja as the room began filling up with the domestic staff of the house. He put the tilak on both their foreheads and gave them prashad. Karan handed Krina a money envelope and said quietly, "Give this to him."

Krina felt shy and uneasy as everyone before leaving the room bowed to the couple. Finally, only the two of them and the pundit were left, and Karan introduced them. "I think you must conduct the morning prayers from now," pundit Banwari Sharma told her. "At whatever time suits you. I will be there, of course." Krina touched his feet and then the two of them left.

"You know, Krina, the morning prayers used to be done by my mother before this," he put his arm around her. "Thank you. I really do love you. I suggest we forget the past and make a fresh start." She nodded shyly, and he said, "It's past 2! Are you hungry? I am!"

In the evening as they enjoyed the beauty of the lawns, Krina asked, "Why did we get married in court?"

"It was my father's decision, because he came to know that you can't travel for another few weeks. He rang up your father and both of them agreed that you couldn't be left alone at your cottage with your nanny. It was better to get married in court and have a wedding reception at Shimla when your parents return from England. Aren't you happy with the decision?"

"Of course I am!"

"It wasn't just our parents, but my wish as well. I couldn't bear to be parted from you any longer. That day in the ICU," his voice was heavy with emotion, "I thought I had lost you."

"Shh, I thought we were making a fresh start," Krina said.

Later that night shivering from the cold outside, Krina shyly stepped into a warm bedroom heated by the fire burning in the grate. Karan stood at the window looking at the sky. The room smelled of his cologne and memories of the night when he had kissed her under the bottlebrush tree came rushing back to her.

As though in a dream, she went up to him. He didn't look at her but put his arm around her and said, "Look at the sky. It's so clear and full of stars. Puranmashi will be upon us in just a few days."

Krina smiled and said, "Yes, but look at that cloud hiding the moon!"

Karan turned to look at her and said, "Just like the cloud that hovered over our union, causing one problem after another. We almost gave up hope, but look at us now; we're together at last."

She sighed and leaned closer into him. He lifted her chin in his hands and kissed her deeply. She put her arms around his neck and kissed him back, forgetting everything else. As their kiss grew more passionate, he lifted her up and carried her over to the bed, her face growing more flushed. He put her down and switched off the lights.

The room was plunged into darkness and the moonlight slowly crept in giving everything a silver hue, but the two were too lost in each other to notice.

# Chapter 16

They were going to visit the temple of Bhawani Ma who came to Karan's grandmother in a dream. She said to go to the site the temple now stands on and dig out her idol from there. The very next day, his grandparents went there, found the idol as predicted, and built the temple.

"You're late," Karan said in the morning as Krina climbed into the back of the open jeep.

"I know," she said apologetically.

He helped her up and said, "Both my parents came to see you when you were unconscious, and my mother had tears in her eyes when she blessed you. She was not at all happy that I had decided to fight for you because it's put your life in danger." He held her hand. "But if it hadn't been for George, I would still be living like a mouse, and you would still hate me. Shallu made me absolutely sick but I had to keep pretending to be in love with her! While you were unconscious, my parents went to the temple to pray for you and made me promise we would visit it once you were better." She smiled and squeezed his hand, and then blushed when he said, "I'm sure Ma will fulfil my parents' desire for a grandson." He smiled at her and told her, "I love you. Don't ever forget."

Bahadur confirmed that everything had been arranged with Ram Singh, and started the car.

Like all the days since she had been discharged, this one, too was clear and bathed in sunshine. The car manoeuvred the narrow, steep road behind the house. The road was lined by bushes, not trees, but it allowed a breathtaking view of the scattered houses in the valley and the stream that snaked through the forested mountain sides. Krina rested her head on Karan's shoulder and enjoyed the view till they reached the temple. It was a white temple with a saffron flag fluttering in the wind, with about twenty or so stone steps leading to it. "Cover your head," he instructed and helped her down, adjusting her woollen shawl.

The roof of the temple was full of men, women and children bedecked in tribal attire and beaded jewellery. As soon as Karan and Krina entered the temple gates, drums, conch shells and pipes sounded all of a sudden. The couple was showered with flowers as they made their way up the stairs.

Karan accepted everyone's greetings with folded hands and a smile. As they climbed, people began singing devotional songs and Karan explained that they were from the Bundi village, which was once part of his family's hill, but then it was given to the family of Sapunde, staunch devotees of Ma.

The temple itself was very small with just about enough space for the priest – the same as the one at Thali house – to sit before a small but beautiful idol of Ma Bhawani, adorned with a red sari and gold jewellery. Both Karan and Krina took a seat on the floor near the door as the pundit began reciting the shlokas. Ram Singh appeared carrying a silver thali covered with a red cloth and placed it in front of the deity. The priest uncovered it to reveal another red sari, more gold jewellery and silver coins, which the pundit arranged on and around the idol. He put tilaks on their foreheads, gave them prashad and blessed them with a son in the near future.

Krina touched the feet of both the pundit and the idol, and as they stepped back out of the door, the devotional songs stopped, and she saw the crowd segregating itself according to gender. As per tradition for the next hour, Karan and Krina stood at the last step and distributed a blanket, one woollen dress, and a box of sweets to the head of each family. The drums, conch shells and pipes started again, and a troupe of men and women began dancing in front of them. They requested the couple to join them so Karan took Krina's hand and danced a little. Much laughter and clapping followed.

Karan told Ram Singh to serve food and drinks to everyone. The *sarpanch* offered a shawl to Karan and a silver beaded necklace to Krina. Both shared some *puris* with the villagers and then left the temple to go back home, even though the celebrations would go on till the night.

In the evening they sat before the fire and Karan began to tell her what had happened when he had left Shimla for Mumbai.

"First, you must know about our family, so before I tell you about what happened in Mumbai, let me tell you about my great-great-grandfather, Thakur Kharak Singh, a *zamindar* and chief of a local tribe. He was known for his integrity, honesty and was a staunch devotee of Bhawani Ma. During the invasion of Tibet by the British my great-grandfather, Thakur Ranbir Singh, helped the British army, but succumbed to the injuries he suffered in the war. The British rewarded our family by giving the title of Raja to my grandfather, Thakur Devi Singh, who was only twenty at the time, added the land from a part of Rampur Bushahr and they declared it the state of 'Thali' because of the mountains around the city and the temple of Shiv below. No one ever tried to invade it because they knew we had the support of the British.

"My grandfather though young and uneducated, was very shrewd. He bought the hill where our hospital and house are and built two hunting houses for the British. Yes, that's what our house originally was. He also extended the Thali boundaries by taking a hill from a small ruler called Thakur Pratap Negi as payment for fulfilling his debts, which began the feud between our two families. He married my grandmother, the only daughter of the Diwan of Bhumi, a small state of Kinnaur. This further added to the strength and wealth of our family, and Thali became one of the most powerful sates in this part of Shimla.

"They had three children: my father was the oldest, Thakur Baldev Singh, my buaji, Kameri Devi, and my *chachaji*, the youngest, Thakur Narinder Singh. Our family was literally worshipped because they were honourable and had no vices and were generally considered shrewd, especially where business was concerned. My father attended the Bishop Cotton School in Shimla. Those were the days when women were not educated above the age of ten, and were made to live under the *purdah*. My buaji was married at the age of eleven to Thakur Prem Singh, the nephew of the ruler of the state of Rampur Bushahr, one of the other biggest and most powerful states. My uncle joined my father at school but dropped out during high school and took to painting. He was a wonderful artist, musician, and poet, so he went to Shanti-Niketan and then to Paris, but came home to marry my *chachiji*, Kumari Shila Devi, the youngest daughter of the courtier of Thali, Thakur Ravi Chand. They had two sons, Kunwar Ravinder Singh and Kunwar Kanti Singh. They went to Bishop Cotton as well.

"My father went to the Mayo College at Lahore, well-known at the time for educating and grooming royalty only. On one of his holidays there he met my mother, Bimla Devi, singing *bhajans* at the Hath-Koti temple. They fell in love and he discovered that she was from the small village in Rampur Bushahr called Sarahan, and the daughter of a priest. When my father completed his education he came home and told my grandparents that he wanted to marry her. They objected but he persevered and soon enough, they were married.

"My father helped my grandfather with the uplifting of the state. They built the Thali palace, which my grandfather named 'Bhawani Palace', though he continued to live in the city palace. My father spoke to the locals and encouraged the business of handicrafts, of woollen shawls and other goods, selling Chalgoza, dry fruit and apples. He aslo built community centres, hospitals and schools for both boys and girls. The annual Lavi fair organised on the 25th of Kartika (November) brought in more business. The fair is said to have started with the signing of a treaty between the ruler of Rampur Bushahr and the Lama of Tibet. I attended that fair once when I was here on vacation during the winter holidays.

"Eight years elapsed after my parents' marriage but they had no child. My grandfather insisted that either my father get a second wife or adopt my chachaji's second son. Initially, my father agreed to the adoption, and since it took six months to complete the process, the papers were readied. However, in December, my mother became pregnant with me and the adoption was forgotten. When I was born, my grandfather abdicated the throne and left with my grandmother to the Thali house. She died of pneumonia when I was five years old, and after her death my grandfather asked my father to move to the Thali house with him.

"Now, the law of primogeniture always brings about some resentment among the younger siblings. My father sent me to Sanawar at the age of five, and when I came back to attend the coronation of my father, I saw my cousin, Kunwar Ravinder Singh, who was by now in high school. The two of us got along very well and he is the one who taught me tennis and horse riding. However, when I was in middle school, I found out that he married a girl called Shallindra Devi of the Negi family against his and my father's wishes. This was a reason for a falling-out between my father and his brother, who accepted my cousin's decision. Shallu had been studying medicine in Delhi, but she gave up her studies and came to live in the city palace. For a while, all was well, but when I went to Boston, I found out that my cousin had been found dead on the bank of the local river Chandra near the village of Gandhla. It turned out that Shallu had encouraged him to indulge in alcohol and had herself gone back to Delhi to complete her studies. He fell prey to other sins as well, and Shallu completely ignored him, spending all her time in Delhi and staying with her own parents during the holidays. My father tried to talk to her but it did not work. So my cousin's death was the first blow to our family. Shallu knew she had to wait a year before she would automatically become the wife of the younger son as per the law, so she took up a job as a doctor in a hospital in Shimla. But by now my other cousin, Kanti Singh had joined the army and refused to marry her. Instead, he married Champa Devi of Kangra when he was posted there for two years as major. She left the palace saying that she wished to do her post-graduation in Mumbai where her brother, Captain Rana Negi, was posted. There was no news of her for a long time.

"The life at Bhawani Palace was comfortable and the abolition of princely states did not affect us. My father became busy in buying and developing hotels at Kasauli, Shimla, Sarahan, a cottage at Fagu near Narkanda and at Hatupeak, and also added a wing in the house called 'Karan Niwas'. He also built a five-star hotel on the hill that had originally belonged to the Negi family. It is a beautiful hotel with an equally beautiful view. From there you can see the view of the three parallel mountain ranges of Zanskar, the greater Himalayas, and the Dhalua Dhars.

"This time when I visited India I found out that my parents had kept from me the condition of my mother's heart. At Thali one day my chachaji and chachiji came with Shallu and her brother. That was my first encounter with them." He laughed as he looked into Krina's eyes. "Now I can see that this talk about Shallu makes you jealous, but you have to know that she fell in love with me only for my wealth, but I'll never have anyone other than my langur." Krina broke into a smile and he continued, "Shallu being a cardiologist advised my father to take my mother to Mumbai for her treatment because they had better facilities.

"Nancy said that she wanted to visit her cousin, Paul, who had married an Anglo-Indian and was now settled in Kasauli. This information was a surprise to me and I agreed to go to with her, and the rest you know.

"Now when we parted and I went to Mumbai, I was extremely surprised to see my father himself waiting for me at the airport rather than his private secretary. He looked very worried. He told me that we were going to Mr Balbir Singh's house for dinner first. He is a criminal lawyer and had been in the same batch as my father in school. My father told me not to worry and asked about you, but then told me what had happened.

"My mother when admitted in Mumbai had to undergo angioplasty. Everything was going fine, but then Shallu came to Mumbai with my buaji and began acting as though she was our most concerned relative. She suddenly suggested that my mother undergoes a bypass surgery, even though there was no need for one. Chachaji came with Shallu's brother to see my mother. My father thought he was just concerned about her so he arranged his stay at the Taj while Shallu stayed at the cantonment with her brother.

"He said that one night my buaji came to tell him after dinner that she had heard my chachaji talking to Shallu and her brother about how you and I were to be married. They mentioned that chachaji still had had Ravinder's adoption papers, which would make him my elder brother, and according to our local custom, it would make Shallu my wife. Then she heard them say something about blackmailing and killing you. My father was shocked and alarmed, and very saddened to hear his own brother plot against him. Do you remember the phone call I received at the hotel?" he asked, and she nodded. "That was my father telling me to come right away. Shallu began acting very clever and attached herself to my mother, but what she didn't know is that my mother always has her wits about her and knows well enough how to manage any situation.

"So we went to the lawyer's house for dinner. He was a very kind and intelligent man, and held my father in high regard. He took my father and me to his office and there we talked. My father explained to him all that had passed. The lawyer listened carefully and asked about the adoption papers. My father said that they were with his brother, but what he didn't know was that they had not been signed by my grandfather because my mother had announced that she was pregnant. Then he asked why chachaji seemed to be so interested. That we did not know, but explained that being the eldest son, my father inherited the main legacy and as per tradition, he gave a third of the rest to his siblings to divide amongst themselves. In our case, chachaji owned the city palace along with some other land and property. After the death of his elder son and his second son joining the army, my father gave him a lot in the form of gifts, but seeing how my chachaji liked gambling and drinking, it was quite possible that he may be in debt and in want of my father's money.

"The lawyer nodded and said that it was a common motive among younger siblings. Then he explained to us that since my grandfather hadn't signed the adoption papers they were not valid, and that the Indian government no longer recognises the rule that provides for the automatic marriage of a widow to her brother-in-law in the case of royalty. Since my chachaji didn't know that my grandfather hadn't signed the papers, the lawyer advised us to keep the pretence up and let him believe that Shallu would somehow marry me. He said that they would try to file a case with the Thali Panchayat to scare us, but there would be no basis for it. The main problem was the blackmail, how they threatened to kill you if I didn't marry her. He offered to call his friend, Mr Kamal Nath, the head of a detective agency to help us out. It was past 10.30pm when the short, fat but very active man in his middle age joined us for coffee, and asked my father the reason for the Negi family's hatred against us. Surprisingly, even I hadn't been aware of the story.

"The hill with the Thali hotel used to belong to a small state, Maithli. The ruler following the abolition of princely states was in a lot of debt, and pledged three hills to my father in exchange for money. Unfortunately for him, he couldn't return the money in time so my father kept the hills and this struck an enmity between them. He had neglected the hills completely, and it was my father who developed them and made a beautiful hotel, and seeing them gain popularity among tourists made him especially angry with us. When my cousin Ravinder fell in love with Shallu, her father apparently told her to make him indulge in alcohol and gaming. My cousin's death was linked to Shallu's brother but the case is still pending.

"So the lawyer again advised us to lie low and go along with the pretence until the detective agency could covertly gather enough evidence against the Negis to convict them," Karan looked at her sadly. "Darling, I had to do what my father said, and it was only done in your best interest.

"Now Shallu was a very clever girl but my buaji was very simple and was easily beguiled. Shallu kept abreast of everything that was happening in Shimla through my buaji. So I gave in and joined the hospital and wrote that awful letter to you, as advised by my father. Then George came and we went to Naldehra where Shallu tried to seduce me when all three of us sat in his room, but George got her so drunk that she ended up exposing herself in a very vulgar way. She fell asleep there and George came to my room, and the two of us talked and left very early the next morning while she was asleep. When she woke up the following morning she was infuriated to find herself in his room and she saw her picture lying half-naked on the bed we had left for her. She was very shameless, however, and followed us back to Shimla. George warned me to protect you. I tried my best but you were very angry with me, and even when we made up, look what happened.

"Now Shallu has been caught because they found her handkerchief in your washroom, her assistant Joseph has also been arrested for attacking you, her brother will be on trial for the attack on at the Mall, and we have doubled our efforts at proving her brother was involved in my cousin's death." He held her and smiled. "Everything is going to be all right."

# Chapter 17

Krina was back to work at the hospital and stood at the window wearing a deep green Pashmina silk dress with a matching shawl over a green skivvy. She looked out at the beautiful valley and sighed with pleasure. She was sure that all their troubles were finally over and that everything would be all right. *If the one you love isn't with you, nothing seems all right,* she reflected as she thought about how unhappy she was without Karan. *Life can't possibly get any better.*

Her gold kangans clinked as she moved her arms and she looked at them and smiled. She had thought all along that her parents had sent them till Karan had asked her, "Who sent you these?"

"My parents," she had replied.

"Are you sure?"

"Of course! How can I possibly forget? My birthday was absolutely awful because you were so horrible to me. I was so upset I didn't even eat the rabri that my nanny had made. The only thing that gave me the strength to go on was coming home to see the presents my parents sent me."

"Really? Why don't you look at the inscription inside?"

Krina had undone the clasp to see the inscription she'd missed. "Oh, Karan, it was you! Oh, I wondered why my parents gifted me jewellery knowing that I don't normally wear any!"

"That day, would you believe, I was actually reprimanded by a junior? Dr Kamlesh told me that I had been too harsh with you when you were sick and too on your birthday, and I realised he was right. I felt terrible and called up our family jeweller who picked these kangans out for you. I had him engrave your name and date of birth on it, and I took it and the chocolates and flowers to your cottage. I left all the presents there for you and also told your nanny to make rabri for you because I know how much you love it. I also asked about your health and told her to give me daily updates. That night she called me and told me that you had gone to sleep without eating anything but were so excited about the kangans that you wore them to bed! Krina, I felt so guilty that day about how I was handling the whole situation that I decided I needed to rethink it and went to George for advice. And I was completely fed up with Shallu. She kept coming over to our house all the time to see buaji, and then she had the cheek to hire an architect to design the cardiology department office that she had claimed her right over. She said she was going to leave Snowdown and she wanted it designed just like mine. I was so furious I told the architect to go on leave till I called him back, and then told Shallu that he had gone on leave because he was sick."

A horn sounded outside and Krina was brought back to the present. She knew it was Karan so she ran out of her office but immediately slowed down as she remembered Karan's words: "You're part of the royal family now, and every action of yours is going to be noticed and commented upon. So talk less to those who serve you and be graceful and dignified in all your actions."

She reached the porch just as he came out of the car to help her in. He got back in next to her and said with a smile, "So, ready to meet your parents-in-law?"

"I'm very nervous."

"Don't be. My parents consider you their own daughter." He instructed Bahadur to take the National Highway to Fagu. "This tunnel we're in, the Sanjauli tunnel, was built in 1851-52 by 10,000 convicts and about 8000 labourers and all were Indians. While it was being built, Lord Kitchner fell off his horse and fractured his leg. The Indians were so scared to touch him that they left him like that for half an hour till help arrived," he chuckled. When they emerged from the 170m long tunnel they were soon on a winding road and exactly 13 km from Shimla where he showed her the palatial red-roofed complex, Wild Flower Hall. It was said to have been Lord Kitchner's house but has now been converted into a hotel, a reminder of the era gone by. "This area has the thickest forest around the periphery of the town. It's very expensive but extremely comfortable to stay for a day or so. All around you can see nature looking so alive and fresh. You feel so…serene. I brought Nancy here for lunch once." He looked at her slyly before continuing, "Now we're close to Kufri, where you went out in the snowstorm and fell ill." The car was now climbing a very steep, narrow road. "There are those snow-covered slopes, a popular tourist spot for those who want to enjoy a bit of skiing. Mahasu Peak is just a short trek away and is a very good picnic spot at 2510m. It's not too high, but in winter snowstorms are very common. There are always some fools who come to watch the snow falling, get caught in a storm, and then end up at our hospital," he winked.

"Very funny."

"We're close to Fagu now. Did I ever tell you about my life growing up in a small town? No? Well, it's quite close to Kufri and just as high, but has its own charm. During the monsoon, the hills and the valley are completely covered in a fog, and from there it gets its name. During our final term, a few of my friends – including your lovely friend Bimla – and I went to the Thali house where they looked around the city. It was when I visited the site where the hospital was to be built with my father that I decided I wanted to be a doctor. The next morning we all went to Fagu where my father slowed down the car and pointed out the beauty of the fog to us, and we stopped for tea at the market. The market is very crowded – mostly with tourists – now, because Fagu is quite a famous place to stay at for a few days because of its serenity and scenic beauty. You'll love it. The only problem is that the weather is very unpredictable, so you can't trek to the top. We went to the resort after exploring the place a little. Our father had booked our stay in one of the only two resorts there, Mahasu Peak. Seeing how beautiful it was there, my father bought a cottage there for us as a weekend getaway. On the manager's advice we went to enjoy the panoramic view of the Himalayas, and visited a small temple near the top. Though the girls didn't come, we walked to Chiyog, or South Fagu, and climbed up to the temple at Tungesh Dhar. I feel Fagu can offer you a view like no other place, and that's why I brought you here. It was at that temple when I touched Devi's feet that I was suddenly reminded of you and all I could think about was that I might be falling in love with you.

"The night we came back to school I couldn't sleep and the next morning I watched you reach for some toast at breakfast. When you saw me staring and you turned bright red and turned your face away from me! I knew there was something different about you, because something about you really touched me. I was so impressed seeing you ride that well and I felt that I must get to know you better but you were very cold to me, so I was hesitant. Suddenly I began wondering whether I was really the same Karan who used to be so bold that he didn't care about what anyone else thought or not. That morning I decided that one day I would bring you to that temple in Fagu."

"I really do want to go there," Krina said.

"Good, because that's where we're going," Karan smiled. The climb to the temple was rather steep and very dark because the trees formed a canopy over the narrow road, blocking out the sunlight. At the top, there was a sudden opening in the trees and some flat land that afforded a magnificent view of the surrounding high mountains and their snowy peaks.

It was sunny and Krina saw animals and temporary Gujjar shelters on the slope. The car drove on, and soon in front of them was a mound with a wooden hut that had a white flag on it, surrounded by cedar trees.

It was nothing but a very small hut with a local deity inside, wearing modest clothes but a gold *nathni*. A priest arrived and recited some Sanskrit shlokas and blessed the couple. He offered them a cup of tea each, and sat down next to them on the stone steps and spoke to Karan who understood the dialect about the temple. The temple was centuries old, built by a Gujjar called Iqbal Singh. The story went that he was sitting at the site of the temple when he fell asleep. A girl came up to him and woke him up. He was angry and was about to scold her when he looked at her more carefully. She was wearing a red *ghagra choli* and a scarf covered her head. She was clearly not from the Gujjar tribe; her fair face with its sharp features and large black eyes told her apart. Furthermore, she was wearing gold nathini, which was unusual for a child of their tribe. She told him, "wake up, dig me out and build me a temple here". He was a very superstitious man and did so, and just as she had predicted, he found her idol. They built a temple that has been immune to the weather and white ants. He converted to Hinduism and became a priest of the Devi."

After visiting the temple they went to Narkanda 40km away, via Theog. "I believe it snowed last night," Karan said, observing the blanched mountains. "Look, there's Pir Panjal. The ski slopes here are very good, much better than at Kufri. Ski season is from January to March. Of course the slopes are nothing like the Alps where one has the company of beautiful girls," he teased.

"Oh I know," Krina said, quite unruffled. "I seem to remember a certain Pamela Scott. Who was she, again?"

"Oh!" Karan laughed. "So George told on me! Let's change the subject then. Would you like some scones?" They stopped at the market for tea before they set out for his cottage, which was on the way to Hatu peak.

"So you really want to know about Pamela?" Karan asked her seriously, and she nodded. "Well, do you remember that girl who called up when we were leaving the Thali house in Kasauli? The truth is that if I hadn't met you by this time, I probably would have married her. I had waited for you so long and my mother, especially now that she was ill, just wanted to see me settled. I met Pamela when George and I had gone to Switzerland for a ski vacation. The very first day, I slipped on the slope and Pamela helped me up. I can't lie; she was very attractive and an excellent skier. For the first time since I had fallen in love with you, I felt something. She was very different from other American girls, and though she came from a very wealthy family, she never showed it. I found myself falling for her and on the last day of the trip, she came to me and confessed that she liked me very much. Before we knew it, we were kissing, but when I looked at her I saw your face, and it was your name, not hers that I whispered. She asked who you were and I had to tell her everything. She was sad but she said she understood, and we parted. The same day I also confided in George for the first time, and he told me about his own experience and that I needed to give it one more year, at least, before I gave up on you.

"She kept in touch with me when I returned to Boston, and when I was about to come back to India, she surprised me with a visit. She told me that she was still in love with me and that if I wanted, she would even move to India with me and change her name to 'Krina' if I liked. I was touched and sorely tempted because I was so angry with you for not making an effort to find me. I told her to call me in India on the 20th of October and I promised her an answer by then. And as you know, she did call and I told her about us. I promise, I forgot entirely about her the moment I saw you in that shop. Though I had ample opportunity, I never cheated on you, because we're only made for each other, and no one else." He held her hand and kissed her softly. "That was the last secret I had that you didn't know."

"Well," Krina said honestly, "I'm just glad that we're finally together."

It had become very dark and the car came to a stop in front of a brilliantly lit house. "This is our cottage. In the morning I shall take you to my favourite place, Hatu peak. I'd really like it if you, too, showed me your favourite places when we go to Dalhousie."

Krina smiled and stepped out of the car. They were greeted by many servants who threw rose petals on them. It was very cold outside but inside the cottage a fire had been lit, making the temperature just right. The cottage was furnished much like the royal Thali houses even though it was much smaller.

"This used to be owned by a major who settled here and opened the first bakery in this part. However, his wife died in childbirth and he went back to Scotland with his newborn son after selling this cottage to my father. He left the structure as it was but redid the interiors entirely. Our suite is upstairs." He gave instructions to a man called Puran Singh regarding dinner and led Krina up the stairs.

The next morning they started the climb to Hatu. Bahadur wasn't driving their car this time, but Krina didn't comment. It pleased her to see Karan so excited to share the place where he'd gown up with her, and she was glad to be a part of his family now.

"No one really drives to the peak," Karan said. "Everyone walks, but because of your health, we have to go by car. It's beautiful if you walk," he said, looking out of the window. It was the Gurkhas who invaded this peak in the nineteenth century and built a fort, which is 5km from our cottage. "The experience isn't considered complete unless you've camped up there. Once my father camped on the ridge and woke up very early to see the magnificent view. We're going to do that together sometime, but only once you're better," he squeezed her hand. "It used to be difficult because the roads were too dangerous to get there and there was no drinking water, but now every year a fair is held and many people go there."

As the 4x4 car climbed up the steep slope, he kept pointing out things he said they would do on their next trip. "We'll be walking through the forest of pines, oaks, rhododendrons, walnuts and deodars. The aroma there is just intoxicating. I know you'll love it."

When they reached the ridge, Krina took in a deep breath and soaked in the whole view.

"If there is heaven on earth, it must be here," he said.

They stopped at the temple of Hatu-Mata where after praying they sat on the stone steps and admired the mountains in silence for a while. Afterwards they drove a few kilometres down from the temple and saw Gujjar settlements where Krina admired the clothes of the tribal women.

"Would you like a dress like that?" Karan asked and she nodded. "You're in luck," he smiled. "Last night I had had one bought for you from the market to attend the function the servants had arranged for us to celebrate our marriage, but you fell asleep."

They had taken a detour because he had to show Krina the Hatu peak. They were now headed towards a rest house in Hat Koti, because his mother had insisted that they visit the temple there. It was shortly after 5 when they arrived but the town already looked asleep. They pulled into the rest house and when they got out of the car, Krina grabbed Karan's arm and said, "Look at that bird! It's a nilgar!"

Karan spotted the nilgar amongst the many birds that broke the town's silence with their chirping. "We royals wear its feather on our turbans, because it is said to be Ma Bhawani's favourite bird."

Unlike the royal cottage the rest house had only very small lawns and its entry through the verandah was not well kept. Some servants, however, did come to receive them and warned them to stay indoors as a snowstorm was expected.

They settled themselves and spent a quiet evening in front of the fire while Karan told Krina about the architecture of the place. "Most of these heritage palaces, temples, old villages here are built on some indigenous material. The kath kani is a unique style of building and it suits to the local climate of hills. The word comes from Kath (wood) and Kani (corner). The walls are raised by creating a wooden mesh with the help of horizontal inter-locking deodar sleepers which are packed with stones and plastered with mud. These buildings remain cool in summer and warm in winter. These are earthquake resistant and deodar is known to bear the catastrophe of any climate for years. However, the roofs are made of wood and covered with slabs of slate stones. I shall show you the typical style of this architecture when we visit the Bhima-kali temple at Sarahan." After dinner Karan spoke about his mother and why she had insisted they go see the Hath-Koti temple.

"She was seventeen when she went there with her parents, my maternal grandfather was a priest who owned an apple orchard at Sarahan – we'll go there before leaving for Thali – at the same time my father was on holiday with his parents at the same place.

That's where my parents met each other and fell in love. They go there at least once every year." He warmed his hands in front of the fire in the grate. Though a storm raged outside, it was very comfortable inside the rest house. "Do you know why turquoise is my favourite colour?"

"It's the colour of Nancy's or Pamela's eyes?" Krina joked.

"No," he replied. "It is the colour of my mother's eyes."

The storm hadn't been too bad so they left the following morning. As they climbed into the jeep, a tall Gujjar man approached them with his wife and children and gave them a ceramic container full of fresh milk. His wife put a beaded silver necklace around Krina's neck while the children watched silently. Krina quickly took off her Pashmina shawl and put it around the shoulders of the woman and pressed some money into her hand. At first she refused to take it but when Krina insisted it was for her children, she reluctantly accepted it.

As she got back into the jeep, Karan took her hand and fondly told her, "Everyday you remind me of why I fell in love with you. You remind me of my mother. You're just like her – tribal, determined but scatter-brained, short-tempered but loving and so generous. And of course, I love your melodious voice and how gracefully you dance." Krina blushed and Karan said, "And this. You will see those same lowered eyes and that shy smile when my father looks at her."

They waved at the family as the car drove off slowly. The road was still wet and slippery but they reached Hath-Koti without incident. The town where the Pandavas were rumoured to have lived during their exile was small and very crowded.

The town of Hat-koti was situated at the junction of the Jubbal and Pabbar valleys where the Bish Kulti rivulet, the Rai nullah and the Pabbar River meet. The temple's complex was scattered over a 5km area. Legend has it that there were two sisters who renounced the world and dedicated themselves to the service of humanity. The elder of the two came to be worshipped as the Goddess Hateshwari Devi, and the temple was built for her. Karan explained to her the structure of this temple: in the seventh or eighth century when it was first built, it was constructed in the Shikara style, but was rebuilt in the nineteenth century by the Jubbal rajas as a two-storey Pagoda made of slate and deodar.

When they entered the temple, they were welcomed by an image of Lord Ganesh at the entrance, along with a large chained "kalash". The main statue in the temple was an eight-armed brass image of Goddess Mahishasur Mardini (an avatar of Durga), on a lion and slaying the demon Mahishasur. There was another beautiful sculpture of her, with an intricately carved body, with fine copper in lay work on the lips and silver on the eyes. The temple was also dedicated to Lord Shiva, whose large lingam adorned the inner sanctum.

"This is where my mother was praying and singing devotional songs in her melodious voice when my father saw her and fell in love at first sight."

Karan went on to point out the magnificent roof of the temple, which had an array of richly carved images of gods and goddesses. They left soon enough. Their final destination for the day was to be Sarahan, with stopovers at Kotgarh, Nirath and Rampur. They were also going to pass through Jubbal, about 14kms away from Hat-koti, a small and beautiful town designed by a French architect in the 1930s.

Kotgarh was the heart of the apple-growing region of Himachal. The history of this place was owed to an American named Samuel Evans Stokes who came to India 1904. He began his sojourn in the hills from Solan's leprosy home, before meditating in a caved and being called Christian Baba. He later moved to Kotgarh and bought apple orchards and married a Christian girl and built a home with her – Harmony House. Karan stopped the driver and told him to turn around because he also wanted to show Krina the Jabber Lake and the famous Nag Devta temple on its bank. It was a small lake against the backdrop of snow-covered mountains and surrounded by weeping willows.

They continued their journey to Rampur but because they had the time, they stopped to visit the sun temple of Nirath 20kms before Rampur, where Bahadur was waiting for them with Krina's Mercedes-Benz.

"Ma's first gift to you: the Benz. It only comes with the condition that you give us an heir," he smiled and put his arm around her as they walked towards the car.

# Chapter 18

When they neared Rampur Karan said, “We’ve taken a detour again, but it’s because I wanted to show you the view. Just look at the snow on those mountains.” Krina craned her neck to get a better glimpse out the window. “We’re almost there. You know, when the King of Bushahr extended his domain down to the Sutlej valley, he shifted his capital to Sarahan first and later to Rampur, naming it Rampur Bushahr. Centuries later when the Gurkhas invaded, the British came to the aid of the king and my great-great-grandfather also helped the British. As thanks for the help, they added more land to our state and made it more powerful. In fact, buaji married the nephew of the ruling royal of Rampur Bushahr. She was a child bride and became a widow at the age of 22.

“There is a Buddhist monastery here – the Dumgir Bodh temple besides other temples dedicated to Raghunath and Narsingji the Vishnu avatar. Also, the biggest fair in the region, the annual Lavi Fair is held here in November to mark the onset of winter and the return of the shepherds from higher altitudes. Woollen tweeds, dry fruit as well as animals are bartered and sold here, attracting people from Lahaul, Kinnaur and even Tibet.”

Sarahan was about 17 kms on the national highway from Rampur, situated at a height of 2165m. On the way, they stopped at Jeori for tea and snacks, a town famous for its milk-based sweet and locally grown plums, peaches and apricots.

When they reached Sarahan it was quite cold. They went to the famous temple of Bhimkali from where Karan pointed out the summer palace of the Bushahrs. Krina noticed how the temple of

Bhimakali architecturally dominated the entire town. She was told that according to Puranas, Sarahan was the place where the ruling king Banasur's daughter fell in love with Lord Krishna's grandson Anirudha. The Shrikhand Peak (the paternal abode of Goddess Laxmi) provided a striking backdrop for this magnificent temple. The three-storied structure was a combination of Hindu and Buddhist styles. It was built of stone and timber. The Pagoda-style building had two big doors, embellished with finely worked silver, which lead to main temple. The intricate relief work on the doors depicted Hindu deities as well as some beautiful detailed pattern of wild flora. Even the balconies and windows had detailed wood carvings. On the first floor there was a temple dedicated to Raghunath and Narsingji where you could also see the image of goddess Bhimakali as a young maiden. On the floor above, there was an image of Shiva's wife Parvati, to whom prayers were offered daily.

The walk to and back from the temple was very pleasant and enjoyable, and Krina was glad for the exercise. They got into the car and were driven to his mother's house where only one of her nephews lived with his family at the time. The car passed through a small but very busy market and stopped by a stream in front of a small yellow house. Bahadur spoke with the man who opened the door and told Karan that his cousin wasn't home, but the man led Karan and Krina inside. There was a small courtyard with a tulsi plant in the middle. The house itself had only two storeys and was made of stone and timber. Pointing at the small Shiva temple, Karan said in a voice heavy with emotion, "This is where my mother grew up, worshipping Lord Shiva. She came back here when after eight years my parents still didn't have a son and my grandfather asked my father to remarry. She prayed to Lord Shiva day and night and finally, I was born. That is the very reason my parents came here while you were sick. They prayed for your health, and I wanted to bring you here to thank Shivaji before we go see my parents." He kissed her cheek. They stayed briefly to have tea and then left for the Thali house.

The sky outside grew dark and the wind howled making Krina glad they were in the safety of the heated car. They reached the Thali house soon, and Krina identified it as the house with the beautiful bougainvillea growing along its boundary walls. They came to a wooden gate that read 'Thali House', which the guards opened for them.

The magnificent lawns gave competition to the other Thali houses, bursting with winter flowers and fruit trees in the distance. It was a white house with a red-tiled roof. "My parents' dream house," Karan told her. "They love each other more and more with the passing of years, just as I'm sure we will." Krina smiled and embraced him.

Yet again, a fleet of servants waited to greet them at the verandah of the house. They walked up the stairs under a shower of marigold flowers and went inside the house. The house's interiors were much like the other Thali houses though this was much smaller. A small corridor led to the sitting room which was lit by chandeliers. Krina immediately went to the bay window and admired the forests as the sun set. The room was comfortably furnished and expensive in taste with heavy oak sofas in blue, red and white. There was already a fire burning in the grate and Karan called her attention to the portrait that hung over it. It depicted a young royal couple holding a child. "This is me at age 1 when ma came to donate money to the temple."

Tea was brought in and Karan asked a servant called Devi Chand to unlock the bedroom. "Only he, myself and now you have access to the bedroom. No one else can enter it unsupervised by Devi Chand," Karan explained. They followed him to the suite where Karan showed her a small sitting room that led to the bedroom. There was a beautiful and heavy set of oak armchairs and above the fireplace was another portrait of his parents. From the bedroom one could see the mountainside with its dense forest, and Karan told Krina, "My parents loved trekking there." While Krina looked around the rest of the room, Karan said, "Come, we have to attend the evening prayers at the Bhima Kali temple."

The temple complex was grand and it glittered, bejewelled by lights under the shadows of the mountains that stood around it like sentries. There was a crowd of people gathered who turned to look at the couple enter. The old pundit, whom Devi Chand called Padama Sharma, received them and the temple bells tolled as everyone began singing bhajans. Karan and Krina took his blessings as he put saffron tilak on their foreheads and gave them Prashad, and hoped Krina would return with a son on her next visit.

Early the next morning Karan woke up to find Krina missing. As he put on his robe he heard the sound of a flute and he parted the drapes to see Krina wearing the dress he'd bought for her while they had been at the cottage, sitting on a boulder surrounded by a few maid servants and their children. He stepped out onto the balcony and listened to her sing to the tune of the flute a little boy played. He looked affectionately at his wife who sat among servants holding a lamb, showing no care for her status, and remembered how much he loved her.

When the song ended all the servants applauded and Krina noticed him. She blushed and walked over to him. He put an arm around her waist and led her back inside.

They left the house to go back to his mother's house to see Karan's cousin. "When I came and stayed with Buaji I went around the old palace with its separate bathing ponds for women and men and well-laid gardens. I loved to stay here and explore the village and its beliefs and traditions." Amidst the tall trees just in the middle of the high mountain was a village called Bhanot. All its fifty houses produced pundits and hence it was called the village of pundits. At the top of the mound on the side Karan pointed out at the white temple with a flag. "That is the temple of *Hari katwarshram Maharaj*. He too was a royal of a small mountain state, who went to Kurukshetra to fight the epic battle in support of the Kauravas. However, his arrival had appeared to Lord Krishna in his sacred vision. Lord Krishna decided to test him and came before him in the garb of a Brahmin, and asked him where he was going. 'I am going to join the Kauravas as an archer.' 'Oh! Show me your skill then,' replied the Lord. Without hesitation, Maharaj used one bow to pierce all the leaves of the pipal tree. Since he was a Brahmin he demanded dakshina from the man, who unwaveringly gave him his head. The Lord was impressed and so blessed the Maharaj so that he would enter Devaloka, the realm of gods and goddesses. This is how he became these people's patron deity."

When they were back on the road to his parents' house he was very quiet and obviously lost in the memories of his childhood. Krina decided not to disturb Karan and got lost in the view from the car.

They stopped at the border post where Bahadur got down from the car and spoke to the guards. They hurriedly came to open the door for Karan who got down as well and shook their hands, accepting their salutes. He spoke to them in Kinnauri while Bahadur fixed the white flags on either side of the car bonnet and the one with their royal insignia in the centre.

For the first time, being part of a royal family filled Krina with a sense of great pride. Karan came over to Krina's side of the car and opened the door. "They want to touch your feet," he said and took out a money envelope from his pocket. "Give this to one of them when they do." She was a little embarrassed by the ritual but did so, and afterwards the barrier was lifted and they passed through.

They were now on a relatively straight stretch between two mountains with a river charging below in the gorge on the left side. Reaching the top, Bahadur stopped the car and they got off. They stood in front of two mountains that bent close together, almost forming an arch. "This is called the 'khirki'. You can see the state of Thali from here. People stop here for good luck." He kissed her forehead and she looked around furtively. "Relax! There's no one here!" he laughed. He put his arm around her and pointed. "This was the capital of Thali but now it's a district town of Himachal Pradesh. Look at that white building. That's the city palace. It now belongs to my uncle." Krina could vaguely make out the shape of towers on either side of the house and a red slate roof. Then on the left, close to the top, she spotted a white temple with a saffron flag. "That's the temple of Ma Bhawani", Karan continued. "Earlier it was only meant for the royal family but now the public has full access to it. One has to climb 108 steps to reach here."

They stood admiring the view for a while and then got back into the car. They drove through a tunnel he said his grandfather had built as a short cut for the people of Thali to fetch fresh water from the river below." To their left appeared an old Hanuman temple. "There was an immediate protest because this temple was in the way, and construction of the tunnel stopped, but he managed somehow to separate the tunnel from the temple, but the people shunned the tunnel and still took the long way around to fetch water. So now this tunnel only connects the city to the palace."

When they emerged from the tunnel they drove through very large gates to the house. The house boasted the largest lawns of all the properties Krina had visited and the most lavish. Her mind boggled seeing all the flowers that bloomed. The car manoeuvred around a black marble fountain, much like the one at the house in Shimla, full of mauve, white and pink lotuses.

It was a grand two-storey house with towers on both sides, and a mountain that stood like a silent sentry in the background. It seemed to Krina like a replica of a palace in London. Krina covered her head when Karan told her, "Krina, here you must remember to appear reserved, talk less, and act dignified. I will be with you at every step."

When they stepped out of the car a band started playing the Thali anthem and they were showered with rose petals as they climbed the steps to the house.

At the door stood both his parents in their royal garb. Karan and Krina touched their feet and Karan's mother welcomed them with the silver thali and tilaks. Karan's father embraced him and with his arm around his shoulder, led him inside. Karan's mother took Krina's hand and led her inside as well, leaving one of the servants to pour oil over the entrance. They walked through the carpeted hallway over which magnificent chandeliers hung giving way finally to a backlit window of cut glass in the centre of the wooden ceiling. "The puja room," his mother whispered to Krina and squeezed her hand. They entered the room guarded by guards in green turbans. It was very well lit and filling the length of one wall was a raised platform of black marble where a 3ft tall idol stood dressed in a red sari and gold jewellery. Next to it were idols of Hanuman and Shiv and Parvati. The old pundit made Krina and Karan sit between Rani and Raja Sahib, and his buaji and her sister-in-law took a seat behind them. The entire hall filled up with ex-courtiers and their wives.

The service lasted about half an hour after which Karan's mother introduced Krina to his buaji. "*Bahu*, touch her feet," Krina did, but instead of blessing her, buaji asked, "But when was the wedding?"

Karan's father quietly told her to have patience and that soon everything would be explained. The family went into the sitting room but buaji's daughter did not follow. Servants entered carrying trays laden with snacks and tea. Krina observed how no one spoke till all the food was laid out. She turned to Karan to say something but he lifted a finger, warning her not to speak.

His father spoke once the servants had left. "Sister, what do I say? It is circumstances that forced me to have Karan marry secretly in court. Don't you remember what you told me in Mumbai? It breaks my heart that my own brother would do something like this but I couldn't risk the lives of my Karan and Krina after the last attempt on Krina's life by the Negi family."

Buaji was clearly surprised. "What?"

He explained everything that had happened to her and she listened with disbelief and horror. "It is a shame," he said sadly. "Our brother was only in it for money. Now he and Shallu and her brother are all in police custody. They have discovered that Shallu and one of her servants attacked Krina in the hospital."

Buaji began crying but Karan's father could only soothe her by saying that he was grateful she had alerted him to the conspiracy and not to worry, because Karan and Krina were both safe, and home.

# Chapter 19

The sun woke Krina up in the morning and lazily she propped herself up on her elbows. Karan wasn't in the room. She went to the window and looked out at the clear day, and the maid entered with the tea, in an expensive china tea-set, and biscuits. Touching Krina's feet she made the tea and handed her the cup very carefully. "Thank you, " Krina said and unconsciously raised her eyebrows when she looked at Karan's side of the bed.

The maid smiled. "Sahib has gone to ride with Raja Sahib." She left the room and shut the door behind her. *He'll never forgo his morning ride, will he?* Krina thought with a smile. She marvelled at the training the servants received, that they understood her every expression.

Her thoughts went back to the previous night when her father-in-law had said to her, "Today I shall tell you something I have never told even my wife, about what I thought when Karan finished school. It was the last day and he sat in the car that I had come to pick him up in and his thoughts were not with me, but with the girl with quiet eyes who he was leaving behind. I recognised the look in his eyes and was reminded of my own love for my wife when we were younger.

"The very same day, I found out who her father was and approached him saying that I needed to talk to him before he left Kasauli. We met the same afternoon but I did not disclose my identity as the ex-royal of Thali. We both laughed at the infatuation we thought you two had developed but we decided to keep in touch because we both felt that it might turn serious. We agreed that the day we would be convinced that you two truly did love each other, we'd allow you to meet.

"For years I felt guilty hiding this secret from my wife but your father and I strongly believed that the female sex is not only unpredictable but also unreliable when it comes to keeping secrets. Both of you were successful in gaining admission to the college in Delhi and it was very cruel indeed for us to separate you two but it was necessary. So I managed to pull some strings and got Karan admission in Boston and after a long talk, he agreed to go and keep his love for you secret.

"Every year your father and I would talk to discuss how matters were progressing, and every year the news was always the same. Your love seemed to grow stronger and stronger. Both our wives began to pressure you two into marriage but we held fast and finally, one year Khanna sahib told me that you were coming back to India and would be in Shimla. I helped him purchase the cottage that you have been staying in, and I got you a job at our hospital. When you and Karan finally got together, we couldn't be happier we finally told our wives the news and needless to say, they were extremely happy as well.

"Since then, of course, you know everything that happened, and I spoke to your father, explaining the situation to him and only once I had his consent did I arrange for the two of you to be married. I promised your father as I promise you that I will not let any harm befall you, and you are now a part of our family.

"I spoke to Khanna sahib recently, he said that they are soon going to return, and he even asked me to help him find a better house in Chandigarh where they will have to live because of your mother's health." He smiled "So, my dear, you have indeed proved to us that your love can never falter. Both of you have our blessings."

Krina sipped her tea by the window as Karan and his father came into view. His mother stopped them to say something, and his father replied she blushed deeply, reminding Krina of herself. All sons love their mothers and constantly look for them in their wives. She smiled at the memory of Karan comparing her to his mother.

They went to visit the Shiva temple in the valley. The four wheel jeep was now driven by a man called Kamal Nath who was driving slowly and carefully because the road along the slope was too narrow. There descent was steep and as they went lower the hillside became rocky with no foliage, ending in a deep gorge. On the way Karan told Krina, "All this land belongs to us. At first it was barren but then my father developed it and also built a hotel there, 'Royal Thali Hotel'. It is a five-star hotel, quite a favourite with tourists, especially foreign tourists. It is busy all year round. If you trek from the back of the hotel to the top of the hill, there at flattened hill top you will find look-out huts built for the tourists to view these mountains, snowy peaks and valley below, and those hills began to be called 'The Whispering Hills'. It was televised and everything, while I was in Boston."

"How so?" Krina asked.

"We're going to find out today." When they reached the temple he said, "It was discovered by Swami Shiva Nanda about thirty years ago and my grandfather built the temple for the *parikrama*. He came to know of a passage leading to a room below built to carry the dead bodies of the royals to the cremation grounds."

Before they entered the temple, however, they went to see a small hut that had now been opened to the public to understand the story behind the name 'The Whispering Hills'. Karan held Kriana's hand and took a seat on the boulders like the rest of the tourists that had gathered to witness the miracle. A sudden chill settled upon them.

Soon enough, two white pigeons fluttered down carrying twigs and entered through a hole in the hut's wall even though the door was wide open. Inside the hut were two graves covered with green cloth. Silence descended on the crowd.

The birds dropped one twig on each grave and then walked around them like a parikrama. They stood for a moment at the foot of the graves and then perched on the roof for a minute before flying away in the direction that they had come from.

The scene that had captivated the audience was over, and everyone dispersed noisily, discussing the strange ritual. Karan pulled Krina up off the boulder and said, "Come, we will hear the true story from the *pujari*." They walked quietly to verandah of the temple where the servants had already arranged cushions for them to sit on. The pujari came up to them clad in a dhoti and took a seat next to them. He spoke very warmly to them and agreed to tell them the story. "My real name was Parmananda Dass. I come from Assam where I finished high school but found that my true interest lay in religion and I became the youngest disciple of Guru Ram Dass. When I spent about ten years with him, I asked permission to leave so I could find solace. I wandered around but had no luck till the day I came to a temple nearby and a pandit gave me shelter. I found my solace and decided to live there. One clear morning I went for a walk to explore the area and chanced upon the rocky, barren hills. The rocks were loose at one spot, I lost my footing and fell God only knows how far down. I lost consciousness and by the time I woke up it was the middle of the night and I was very thirsty so I tried to go to the stream I could hear nearby, but I was so badly wounded I could barely move. I was so tired I could do little other than lay there. The next morning at dawn a man from the Gujjar tribe named Talib found me and nursed me back to health. He took me to what I had thought was a cave, but really was a small, forgotten Shiva temple. It was overgrown with weeds and bushes that the structure had almost entirely collapsed, but the lingam remained undisturbed. I was so engrossed in my effort to retrieve the lingam that I didn't even notice when the man left. I decided to devote myself to Shiva at that very temple and lived on the fruits and berries in the forest and water from the stream. No one came to that valley, neither man nor animal, except one day a forest official found me and found his true calling and became my disciple. Soon the servants of the palace found out and the old Raja Sahib came to visit the temple and had it reconstructed.

"I was reminded of that young Gujjar and wanted to see him again so I went to the tribe to look for him, but no one had even heard of him. I met the chief of the tribe and told him the story, and in return he told me that the place I had fallen from was called 'Black Hill' because there had been a landslide once, killing an entire Gujjar settlement called Gonda. Since then no one had ever ventured down into the small valley. But he did know of the man I spoke about. He told me that the hill was haunted. Once, long back, a prince got separated from his men on the hill and found the Gujjar tribe where he fell in love with a girl, Gulabo. He married her and took her back to his state, but was disinherited by his father who was furious with him for marrying so low beneath his status. So he returned with his wife to the village and they lived together for a short while until she fell off the same hill that you did, but she died. Her father buried her very close to the temple. The prince built a thatched hut for his wife and her grave was hidden from view, protected by the trees. He did not survive her by many days, and when he died, he was buried next to her.

"Soon the hut was forgotten until new roads were paved and more and more people began to come to this temple. One day after dark someone saw a light in the hut and they swore they saw a man and a woman emerge from it. The couple sat by the lake while the woman sang in her melodious voice and then they returned to the hut and there was darkness all around once again.

"The rumour spread around the community that this place was haunted and people stopped coming here again. Six years ago in the month of November it had been snowing and one night a tall foreign man found this temple, half dead. His head had been injured and it was bleeding profusely. I took care of him till we could get some help, and about a week later he came back asking if he could live in the verandah for some time. I was extremely puzzled but agreed and he promised me that he would explain everything if he discovered that he was right.

"Every day he would sit with his notebook taking notes and roamed the valley. He even started spending a lot of time by the hut, sometimes even sleeping there. A long time passed and finally, he said he was going to explain everything. One day he took me to the hut, seated me on a boulder and told me to wait. We waited for what seemed like hours and finally, we felt a strange cold breeze and a pair of white pigeons with twigs in their beaks came flying to the hut. They both went in through the hole in the wall and then came out without the twigs.

"It was all very dramatic. The man left but came back soon with a film crew and a forest official who broke down the hut's door. Inside were the two graves you see now, covered entirely by twigs that the pigeons had been placing. The film crew set up their cameras and they recorded exactly what you witnessed today. They broadcasted the documentary and that reporter gave this place the name of the 'Whispering Hills' of Thali. He went to the palace the prince was from and confirmed that he was the same man buried in the grave." The pujari grew quiet as he carefully watched the couple that had listened attentively all the while. "Do you believe in reincarnation of lovers? Do you believe that they are destined to be together in every lifetime?"

"Yes," Krina replied. "Karan and I were separated and we have finally been brought together after so many years and I know that we will be together in our next life, too."

The pujari closed his eyes and smiled. "You two were the prince and the Gujjar girl in your previous lives. These pigeons will stop coming once their time comes and they take rebirth." He got up and said, "Let me show you the tunnel through which you can go see the Nag temple and receive your blessings. If you're lucky, you'll be blessed with a little one soon."

Still unable to come to terms with the fact that they were the two lovers the pujari had told them about, Krina and Karan followed him incredulously.

The pujari led them down a dark passage with the help of a lamp and Karan held Krina's hand tightly as they walked over the damp stone floor. At the end of the passage they came out into a dark, empty room with a bamboo curtain on one side, which the pujari drew aside and opened the wooden door with a silver latch that it screened. It opened into the royal tunnel. "It starts from the puja room in your house," he told them. "This is the coronation room," he said, leading them to it. "Here is where the new king is crowned. You were too young to remember your father's coronation, but I was there. The pandit performed the puja and I blessed him. Your grandfather was bathed in water from the Ganges and wrapped in white silk with his feet exposed to show humility, that he came into this world with nothing, and he left with nothing, while your father was dressed in his royal robes, crown and jewelled sword. After the ritual, the rest of their relatives came in and your grandfather was carried off to the crematorium." He led them there. They were too choked with emotion to speak.

They emerged from the tunnel and were by the lake again where they saw the Nag temple. They went to pay their respects and ask for blessings, and Krina caught the eye of a man standing on the black marble steps, smiling at her. They bent down to touch the pujari's feet but as she bent down, Krina suddenly felt dizzy, lost her balance and was caught by Karan as she blacked out.

When she opened her eyes she was back at the palace and the worried faces of her parents-in-law looked at her. "Are you all right?"

Karan stood next to the doctor who was wreathed in smiles. Somehow, she understood that smile and in an instant, knew. A furious blush crept up to her cheeks as she thought *I'm going to be a mother*. The last thought she had before losing consciousness was of that strange man on the black marble steps with his mischievous smile.